TRUE CRIME CASE HISTORIES

VOLUME 9

JASON NEAL

AKAMAI PUBLISHING

Cover photos of:

Daniel Holdom (top-left)

Susan Barnes Carson / Suzan Bear Carson (top-right)

Justina Morley (bottom-left)

John Joubert (bottom-right)

More books by Jason Neal

Looking for more?? I am constantly adding new volumes of True Crime Case Histories. The series **can be read in any order,** and all books are also available in paperback, hardcover, and audiobook.

Check out the complete series on Amazon

https://amazon.com/author/jason-neal

or

JasonNealBooks.com

**FREE Bonus Book
For My Readers**

**Click to get
your free copy!**

As my way of saying "Thank you" for downloading, I'm giving away a FREE true crime book I think you'll enjoy.

https://TrueCrimeCaseHistories.com

Just click the link above to let me know where to send your free book!

Choose Your Free True Crime Audiobook

Add Audible Narration and Keep the Story Going!
Plus Get a FREE True Crime Audiobook!

Switch between listening to an audiobook and reading on your Kindle.
Plus choose your first audiobook for FREE!

https://geni.us/AudibleTrueCrime

CONTENTS

Introduction xi

1. World's Worst Mom 1
2. The Murder of Stephanie Hebert 17
3. The Eagle Scout 29
4. Baby Lollipops 45
5. Pied Piper of Tucson 57
6. The Slumber Party 71
7. Beyond Redemption 77
8. Rat in the Oven 91
9. A Tragic December 105
10. The Count 117
11. Angelic 127
12. The Bears 139
13. Bonus Chapter: The Family Murders 153

Online Appendix 173
Also by Jason Neal 175
Free Bonus Book 177
Free Audiobook 179
Thank You! 181
About the Author 183

INTRODUCTION

If you're a fan of true crime, you're undoubtedly familiar with the big-name cases; Ted Bundy, BTK, David Berkowitz, Christopher Watts, Diane Downs, Casey Anthony, Jeffrey Dahmer, Jodi Arias, Ed Gein, etc. The list of well-known, notorious cases throughout history is seemingly endless. Books, websites, podcasts, streaming television series, and magazines are filled with their abhorrent tales of mayhem. They're some of the most diabolical killers the world has ever known.

Some killed just for the thrill of it, others were blinded by fits of jealousy. Some murdered for greed, custody of children, or insurance payouts, while still others just wanted to know what it felt like to end a person's life. Of course, mental illness plays a part in countless murders.

In my books, I do my best to find stories you may not have heard of. Of course, for some ardent true crime fans, that's a difficult task. However, my goal is for the vast majority of readers to learn of something new – to read a story that they've heard nothing about.

That's specifically why I ask my readers to send story ideas to me. The cases I find most interesting are the ones I've seen nowhere on the internet, when I have to dig deep to find any information at all. I thrive on the research. To those of you that sent story ideas in the past, thank you so very much. Please send more. I look forward to receiving your emails with new cases to look into.

Several readers submitted stories found in this volume, including the story of five-year-old Stephanie Hebert, who walked only three houses down her quiet suburban sidewalk and disappeared forever. Her case went cold for forty years before other children from her neighborhood came forward in their adulthood with information leading to the killer.

Several other stories in this volume were submitted by readers and I've slated even more to be featured in the upcoming volumes of True Crime Case Histories.

If you'd like to submit a story that you remember from the past that has received little media attention, please email it to me. I'd love to see what details I can uncover. You'll find my email address at the end of this book.

———

In this volume, you'll read twelve assorted true crime stories ranging in date from the 1950s to 2020.

There's the story of the sadistic mother who viewed her children only as the spawn of their demon father, torturing them for the entirety of their short lives.

You'll also read of the deranged husband and wife team who started their own cult and made it their life's mission to rid the world of witches.

Another story tells the disheartening tale of a toddler's skeleton found in a suitcase on the side of the road. Motorcyclists discovered her mother's skeleton more than 600 miles away. Five years had passed with no one having ever realized they were missing.

———

Watching the news, one might think that violent crime is on the rise. Hell, watching the news, one might think the whole world is coming to an end – but it's not. According to recent research, violent crime has been on a steady decline since its peak in the early 1990s.

Granted, the serial killers of the 70s and 80s have morphed into boys with AR-15s shooting up schools and grocery stores, but overall there really is less killing going on in the world. We need to remember that. It's easy to see how one might think things are getting worse. With 24-hour television news and endless news feeds following us all around on the internet, we see much more coverage of murders today than we did during the one hour of nightly news we had in past decades. I just want to remind my readers that the world isn't really going to hell in a handbasket.

Although we may never truly understand what goes on inside the mind of a killer, by studying the cases and knowing their backstory, at least we might gain a little insight into what makes them tick. With any luck, we can learn from the past.

———

Lastly, please join my mailing list for discounts, updates, and a free book. You can sign up for that at

TrueCrimeCaseHistories.com

You can also purchase paperbacks, hardcovers, and signed copies of my books directly from me at:

JasonNealBooks.com

Additional photos, videos, and documents pertaining to the cases in this volume can be found on the accompanying web page:

https://TrueCrimeCaseHistories.com/vol9/

Thank you for reading. I sincerely hope you gain some insight from this volume of True Crime Case Histories.

- Jason

CHAPTER 1
WORLD'S WORST MOM

In June 1984, Maybel Harrison drove along California State Route 89, northwest of Lake Tahoe, as the first hints of sunrise began to glow against the Sierra Nevada mountains. As she passed the Squaw Valley ski resort, she saw bright yellow flashes through the trees on the side of the road. Something was burning. Curious, she stopped the car and climbed down the sloped roadside to get a closer look. What she saw horrified her. A body was burning on top of what seemed to be a makeshift funeral pyre.

Maybel ran back to the highway and flagged down a trucker, who used his CB radio to alert the Placer County Sheriff. When authorities arrived and extinguished the fire, they found the body of a young woman burning on top of a heap of clothing and miscellaneous personal items. The woman appeared to be about twenty years old. Her legs and arms were bound and duct tape covered her mouth. Her body was almost entirely charred. Her cheeks and the backs of her calves were the only parts of her body that hadn't been burned.

In the heap beneath her body, investigators found pieces of clothing, jewelry, and a toothbrush but no identification at all.

The body and the clothing had all been soaked with gasoline. Investigators were puzzled, however, when disposable diapers were found at the scene. There was no sign of a baby and an autopsy later revealed that the woman had never given birth.

Further examinations of the body showed that the girl had been severely abused over a long period of time and there was a large puncture wound on her back. However, neither the wound nor the abuse had killed her. The woman's lungs were filled with soot, indicating that she had been alive when she was set on fire, but it wasn't the fire that had killed her. She had died of smoke inhalation. Investigators searched dental records and examined what was left of her fingerprints, but there was simply no record of the girl.

A composite drawing was created based on what was left of her face and released to the media, but months went by without any clues as to her identity. From that point forward, the girl was only known as Jane Doe #4858-84.

———

Eleven months later, just six miles from where the first Jane Doe was found, a man walking in the Martis Creek Campground noticed a large box in some bushes not far from the road. When curiosity compelled him to open the box, he found the body of another young girl.

Again, investigators found no identification at the scene and no missing person reports matched her description. The second girl had died of dehydration and starvation. She, too, showed signs of severe abuse. The second girl became known as Jane Doe #6607-85.

Although the bodies were found near each other, the second body was found across county lines in a different jurisdiction and the two cases were not connected. It would be almost a decade before anyone would come forward with any information about the two murders.

———

More than eight years had passed since the two bodies were found and twenty-three-year-old Terry Knorr's horrific secrets had eaten at her for as long as she could remember. She needed to tell someone. Anyone that would listen. But when Terry told Utah police what she knew, they brushed her off. So did her therapist. It was an insane story. It couldn't possibly be true.

In late October 1993, Terry Knorr called 1-800-CRIME-TV, the phone number for the television show America's Most Wanted. She knew they would listen. The TV show operators put her in contact with detectives in Placer County, California, where the first body had been found. Finally, she had found someone that took her seriously.

Terry shared with detectives her lifetime of horrific abuse at the hands of her sadistic mother, which led to the death of her two sisters, Suesan and Sheila Knorr. In less than a month after her phone call, the two Jane Does had been positively identified as her sisters and authorities had arrested her two brothers and her mother, Theresa Knorr.

———

Theresa Knorr was born Theresa Cross in 1946 to Jim and Swannie Cross. By her early teenage years, Theresa's father had developed Parkinson's disease and was no longer able to work, leaving her mother to raise the family. Theresa was very close to her mother. When she was just fifteen, however, while Theresa was buying groceries with her mother, Swannie Cross collapsed and died in her arms.

Her mother's death hit Theresa hard. With her father unable to work, the family had no income and were forced to sell the home they had lived in. Theresa fell into a deep depression and grasped for anyone to love her. At just sixteen years old, she dropped out of high school and married her first boyfriend, twenty-one-year-old Clifford Sanders.

Ten months after their wedding, Theresa gave birth to her first son, Howard Sanders. Their young marriage, however, was already having trouble. Theresa suffered relentless mood swings. One minute she would be a kind and loving wife, the next moment she was angry and accusatory. She complained that Clifford drank far too much and was insistent that he was having sex with women he had met in bars. In June 1964, after Clifford spent a night out drinking with friends, Theresa berated him when he finally returned home. The argument that ensued resulted in Clifford punching her in the face. Theresa reported the assault to the police but refused to press charges against her husband. Perhaps she had second thoughts – or another plan.

Less than a month later, Clifford spent his birthday out with friends rather than home with Theresa, who was now pregnant with their second child. Early the next morning, July 6, 1964, she confronted him and again accused him of infidelity. Clifford responded to the accusation by saying what had been on his mind for quite some time. He wanted a divorce. The news was more than she could take. Theresa flew into a jealous rage, grabbed a rifle, and shot him as he walked out of the back door.

Clifford had raised his hand to deflect the shot, but the bullet pierced his wrist, entered through his chest, and continued directly into his heart. It killed him instantly. At just eighteen, Theresa was charged with the murder of her husband.

During her murder trial, Theresa testified that Clifford Sanders was an abusive alcoholic and she had killed him in self-defense. She cried as she told the court that she had grabbed the gun only intending to threaten him. She only wanted him to stop hitting her. She claimed the gun had accidentally fired.

Although there was no evidence of bruising or other signs of physical abuse on her body as she had claimed, as well as an autopsy of Clifford's body that revealed there was no alcohol in his system at the time of his death, the jury couldn't say no to the poor, young, pregnant girl. She was acquitted. After the trial, several of the jurors came up to her and hugged her, expressing their satisfaction that she was finally rid of "that horrible man."

The day after her acquittal, Theresa brazenly showed up at the District Attorney's office, demanding they return the rifle that had been used as evidence against her.

The following March, Theresa gave birth to her second child, Sheila, and began dating Robert Knorr, a Marine Corps private. Knorr had done a tour in Vietnam where he was shot on two different occasions and had also a bridge blown up beneath him. The three incidents left him with severe injuries that had required several months of recovery in a military hospital.

Within months of meeting Robert Knorr, Theresa was pregnant again. On July 9, 1966, she and Robert Knorr were married. That September she gave birth to her third child, Suesan Knorr, and the couple had two more boys in quick succession, William and Robert Jr. Knorr.

Due to his injuries in Vietnam, Robert Knorr's subsequent job opportunities with the military were limited. Restricted to light duty, he was assigned as a funeral escort which required travel all over the country. When young men returned from Vietnam in body bags, Robert Knorr was there to carry a casket or shoot a rifle into the air as part of a twenty-one gun salute.

With her husband gone for several days at a time, it left Theresa home to take care of five children. Again, her imagination went wild. Like she did with her first husband, Theresa accused Robert of infidelity.

As her anger festered, Theresa aimed her aggression at her children, abusing them physically, verbally, and psychologically. By late 1969, Theresa was pregnant a sixth time but her marriage with Robert was collapsing quickly. She was prone to frequent outbursts of anger and accusations and Robert couldn't take another day of what was to become the onset of her borderline personality disorder. With Theresa seven months pregnant, the two divorced in June 1970.

Sheila Sanders / Suesan Knorr / Theresa Knorr

Two months after the divorce was finalized, Theresa gave birth to a girl, Terry. However, when Robert came to visit the children, she refused to allow him access. From that point on, Robert was no longer allowed to see his children.

The following year, Theresa Knorr married once again. This time, however, the accusations of infidelity flew from both her and her new husband from the very beginning. They were divorced within a year.

Theresa spent the next four years drinking at the American Legion Hall in Rio Linda, California, and often left her children home alone for days at a time. In August 1976, she met and married Chet Harris after having known each other for only three days. Chet was almost thirty years older than Theresa. Although she quickly grew to hate him, he and her daughter, Suesan, grew close, which angered her even more. After less than four months of marriage, she had divorced once again.

The final divorce changed Theresa dramatically. She drank more and more, gained a tremendous amount of weight, and became increasingly anti-social – so much so that she got rid of the telephone as she didn't want to speak to anyone and wouldn't even allow the children to have friends over. Unfortunately, the change that the children noticed most was at the level of abuse. To Theresa, the children were the spawn of the devil, Robert Knorr, so they deserved to be punished.

As her level of drinking escalated, so too did her mania. She often threw kitchen knives or scissors at the children and once put a gun to the head of her youngest daughter, Terry, as she threatened to kill her. Beatings occurred almost daily. The children were burned with cigarettes and force-fed until the point of vomiting. When they vomited, she made them eat that too. Theresa ordered her children to hold the others down when it was time for a beating, with the boys often ordered to participate in the beating of their siblings or face a beating themselves.

The girls received the bulk of the abuse, especially Suesan. Theresa's delusions grew more and more insane. She truly believed her girls were demons. As Theresa got older, fatter, and uglier, the young girls, reaching their teenage years, became more beautiful. Theresa, who had once been young and attractive, was convinced the girls had cast a spell on her: they were stealing her beauty and causing her to gain weight.

Howard, the oldest son, was the lucky one. He managed to get away from the madness. He left home when the family moved to a run-down trailer park on Auburn Boulevard in Sacramento in 1983, just before the real insanity began.

The new neighborhood was known for seedy motels, street prostitution, heroin addicts, and drug dealers. But even in a neighborhood like that, the Knorr family stood out. Neighbors noticed that their two-bedroom apartment smelled of urine and the children were rarely let outside of the house.

In 1980, fifteen-year-old Suesan Knorr was picked up on the streets of Sacramento. She had run away from home and was trying to survive as a prostitute. Suesan was caught by a truancy officer and placed in a psychiatric hospital. In the hospital, she told of the extreme abuse that she had received from her mother. However, when authorities confronted her mother, Theresa denied any accusations of abuse. The other children backed up their mother's lie, knowing they would be beaten if they didn't. Theresa assured authorities that Suesan had mental problems and often made up crazy stories. Without further investigation, Suesan was returned to the custody of her mother.

Scared to death, Suesan returned home and prepared for the worst. Theresa donned heavy leather gloves to protect her fists as she punished her daughter with a brutal beating. Suesan's siblings were all ordered to take part in the beating as well, passing around the leather gloves until they were covered with Suesan's blood.

For her defiance, Suesan was handcuffed beneath the kitchen table and the other children were ordered to watch over her to make sure she didn't escape. From that point on, none of the children ever went to school again. Theresa had told their previous school that they had moved out of the school district but never bothered to enroll the children in a new school. Most of them never made it past the eighth grade.

Suesan was kept secured under the table for the next two years. The gag in her mouth was only occasionally removed when her mother hand-fed her. When Suesan rebelled, she was force-fed to the point of vomiting. Theresa, of course, made her eat that too. By 1982, Suesan's will had broken and her mother removed her handcuffs. She was finally allowed to sleep with the other children.

Despite her abuse, Suesan was still the only child that had been brave enough to stand up to their mother – but her defiance continually made her a target. During an argument in June 1983, Theresa flew into a manic rage and ordered her sons to hold Suesan still while she pulled out a gun and shot her daughter in the chest.

Suesan slumped and bled out on the floor, but she was still alive. Barely. The bullet had missed any vital organs but had lodged in her spine. Theresa ordered the children to handcuff Suesan and lay her in the bathtub, where she stayed for almost two months as her mother nursed her back to health. The children were ordered to tell no one.

Miraculously, Suesan recovered. When she was well enough, Suesan begged her mother to let her leave the home to make a life on her own and, surprisingly, Theresa agreed. But her freedom would come with one stipulation – she needed to have the bullet in her spine removed. Theresa didn't want there to be any evidence that she had shot her daughter.

In July 1984, Theresa Knorr prepared for an amateur surgery in the home. She gave Suesan a heavy dose of Thioridazine (a drug to treat schizophrenia) and a bottle of whiskey, then had her lay on the kitchen table. The drug and alcohol cocktail knocked Suesan unconscious and the surgery began.

Theresa handed her son, Robert Jr., an X-Acto knife and ordered him to dig into her back to look for the bullet. Robert dug deep into his sister's back with the knife and probed with his fingers to find and remove the bullet. The surgery was a success. But, when Suesan finally woke, her pain was excruciating. Theresa fed her antibiotics and ibuprofen to ease the pain but they only seemed to make her condition worse. Within days, Suesan's eyes had turned yellow and she was no longer able to control her bowels. Internal bleeding caused massive black bruises on her back. Suesan then slipped into a coma.

On July 16, 1984, Theresa filled plastic garbage bags with all of Suesan's belongings. Every piece of clothing she owned, every photo of her, anything that proved she ever existed went into the garbage bags. She then ordered William and Robert Jr. to put a diaper on their sister, duct tape her mouth shut, and carry her to the trunk of the car.

Composite drawing of Suesan Knorr / Robert Knorr Jr. / William Knorr

The family left Sacramento with Suesan in the trunk and drove east until they reached Highway 89. They drove south through the night along Highway 89 and pulled over near the banks of Square Creek. Theresa carried the garbage bags with Suesan's belongings to an area near the creek bed while the boys carried their sister and laid her on top of the trash bags. Theresa then doused her daughter and her belongings with gasoline, lit a match, and walked away.

———

It didn't take long before all the anger and insanity that had been directed at Suesan was directed at Sheila. Theresa had been drawing unemployment but found a new way to supplement her income: she forced twenty-year-old Sheila onto the streets into a life of prostitution.

Life as a prostitute horrified Sheila, but it seemed to please Theresa. The money Sheila brought home was much more than her unemployment payments. As a result, Sheila was allowed to leave the house as she pleased for short periods of time and received fewer beatings.

But by May 1985, everything changed. Theresa contracted a sexually transmitted disease – worse, she believed she caught it from using the toilet after Sheila. She also accused Sheila of allowing herself to get pregnant during her sex work.

Sheila was gagged, her feet were bound, and her hands were tied behind her back. Theresa, William, and Robert Jr. beat Sheila within inches of her life. They then placed her into a small linen closet measuring only sixteen inches by twenty-four inches. The shelving of the closet made it even smaller. There was only room for her to stand. She couldn't kneel, sit, or even turn around. Though the children could hear grunting and moans coming from the closet, they were strictly forbidden to open the door under any circumstances. No food, no water, no bathroom. Nothing. When the noises coming from the closet got too loud, Theresa would just turn up the television.

After three days in the closet, the family heard a loud thud. Still, Theresa insisted that none of the children open the closet door. After another three days, however, the smell was too much to stand. When they opened the door, Sheila's decomposing body was curled up on the floor. She had died of starvation and dehydration.

———

Theresa filled a large cardboard box with blankets and the boys placed Sheila's body into the box. They then put the box in the trunk and again drove through the night toward Lake Tahoe. Theresa instructed the boys to dump the box next to some bushes near the banks of a small lake in Martis Creek Campground. Just a few hours after they dumped her body, a man found the box and alerted the police.

———

For the next three months, the family could still smell the unmistakable odor of decomposition lingering in the house. Theresa was convinced that the smell alone could implicate her in the death of her daughter. On September 29, 1986, the family packed their belongings and moved out. However, sixteen-year-old Terry was ordered to go back to the apartment, douse it in lighter fluid, and set it on fire. She did as she was told, but the three containers of lighter fluid weren't enough to do much damage. Neighbors quickly called the fire department and most

of the apartment was left intact, including the closet where
Sheila had died.

Terry knew that she would be the next target of her mother's
rage – both of her sisters had warned her. Rather than go into
hiding with her mother and brothers, Terry ran away. She had
kept Sheila's identification card and spent the next several years
posing as her sister.

After leaving the Sacramento home, twenty-four-year-old
William also cut ties with his mother and moved in with his
girlfriend. Robert Jr. stuck by his mother's side and the two of
them moved to Las Vegas.

Robert Jr. and Theresa Knorr kept a low profile in Las Vegas for
years until November 7, 1991, when Robert attempted to rob a
bar and ended up killing the bartender. He was convicted of
murder and sentenced to sixteen years in prison. Immediately
after her son's arrest, Theresa moved to Salt Lake City, Utah,
where she started using her maiden name and got a job as a
caregiver for an elderly woman.

———

Almost nine years had passed since Sheila's death when Terry
Knorr and her new husband decided to call the America's Most
Wanted hotline.

When Terry told police the horrific story, they revisited the
evidence recovered from both of the Jane Doe scenes. Fingerprints were lifted from the box in which Sheila's body had been
discovered. The prints matched both William and Robert Jr.
The box was traced back to a movie theater where William had
once worked.

William Knorr was still living in the Sacramento area and worked in a warehouse when he was arrested. When questioned, he initially denied everything. However, when detectives laid out the evidence against him, his brother, and his mother, he admitted his guilt. Robert Jr. was brought from his prison cell in Nevada back to California to face charges. He, too, initially denied involvement but later admitted his guilt.

Theresa Knorr had been tracked down via a driver's license application she had filed in Utah. Just five days before her arrest, she had been arrested for driving under the influence of alcohol. When officers showed up at the address on her driver's license, she was already packing her bags. She knew the police were looking for her. When questioned by detectives, she refused to cooperate and immediately requested legal counsel.

Theresa Knorr was charged with two counts of murder, two counts of conspiracy to commit murder, and two special circumstances charges: multiple murder and murder by torture. She initially pleaded not guilty but later changed her plea when she was told that her son, William, was planning to testify against her. Her guilty plea eliminated the chance that she would be sentenced to death.

On October 17, 1995, Theresa Knorr was sentenced to two consecutive life sentences. She will be eligible for parole in 2027 at the age of eighty.

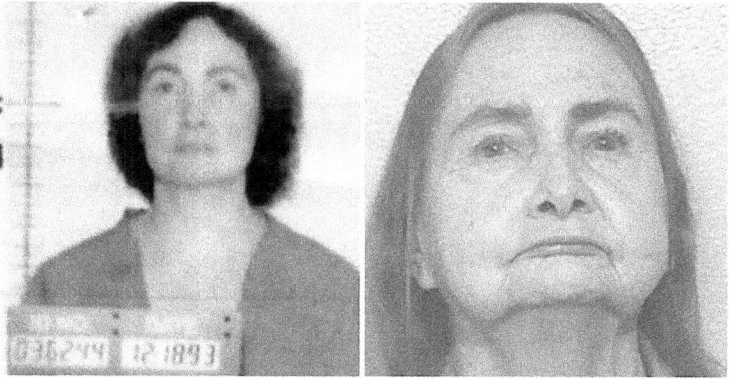

Theresa Knorr - at time of arrest & more recent photo.

Although the boys had pleaded guilty, the circumstances of their involvement in the murders of their siblings were not cut and dry. Their lifetime of abuse and constant threat of further abuse clearly influenced their involvement.

For his role in the murders, William Knorr was sentenced to probation and ordered to undergo psychological therapy. Robert Knorr Jr. received an additional three years concurrent to his existing prison sentence for the bartender's murder. After his release from prison, Robert Jr. was arrested again in 2014 on multiple child pornography charges. He is due to be released in 2024.

Terry Knorr died of a fatal heart attack in 2011. She was forty-one years old.

CHAPTER 2

THE MURDER OF STEPHANIE HEBERT

W aggaman, Louisiana, sits along the west bank of the Mississippi River, just eighteen miles upstream from New Orleans. In the mid 70s, the new subdivision of Floral Acres seemed like a nice place to raise a family. Just a few hundred feet from the Mississippi, young children climbed the jungle gym in the large playground within the subdivision and parents felt safe letting their kids freely play in the suburban streets. Unfortunately, hindsight would later prove that the unassuming suburban neighborhood was anything but safe.

———

Even though five-year-old Stephanie Hebert had just spent the night at her friend Lorie's house the night before, she couldn't wait to go back to Lorie's the next afternoon. They had plans to play all day. It was early June 1978 and Stephanie was excited. Summer had finally arrived and in just a few short months, she would start first grade. Lorie lived only three houses down on Aster Lane. Her mother called to her, "Be back for dinner at 5:30," as Stephanie ran out the door and down the sidewalk.

Joyce Hebert wasn't concerned when Stephanie didn't show up for dinner. Why would she be? Stephanie was only three houses away. She was obviously just busy playing and lost track of time. But when Joyce walked to Lorie's house to retrieve her daughter, the terror hit her. Stephanie wasn't there. In fact, she hadn't been at Lorie's at all that day. She had never made it just the few steps down Aster Lane.

Stephanie Hebert

Stephanie's mother notified police right away and an extensive search began for the blonde-haired, blue-eyed little girl. When Stephanie left the house she had been wearing a pink checkered top, a pink skirt, flip-flops, and her baby-blue glasses. More than 150 sheriff's deputies and countless volunteers searched the neighborhood and nearby woodland. The search included canals and drainage ditches that cut across the marshland and levee near the river, but there was no trace of Stephanie.

————

By the next morning, the disappearance of Stephanie Hebert was front page news throughout the area. Everyone was on the lookout. That evening, a woman who sold ice cream and cotton candy from a truck just blocks from Stephanie's home called police. She told detectives that around 5:00 P.M. on the day she went missing, she saw Stephanie. The woman was certain it was her. She recalled her blonde hair, pink checkered top, and her light blue glasses. The woman claimed Stephanie was holding the hand of a middle-aged woman with dark brown hair and heavy makeup. She sold them two cotton candies and Stephanie appeared to be smiling and happy. The woman recalled that the two of them left in a dark blue 1974 Pontiac Trans Am, but that was the last she saw of them.

A full week had gone by with no sign of Stephanie when the police received another tip. Another witness claimed to have seen Stephanie and the dark-haired woman. This time, a man told detectives that moments ago he had seen them getting on a city bus crossing the river away from New Orleans. Police rushed to stop every city bus in operation and searched for Stephanie and the mystery woman, but they had no luck.

Police received dozens of tips daily and each one was checked out thoroughly, but none led to any sort of clue. Detectives believed that Stephanie had been kidnapped and some sort of ransom request would eventually surface, but the days passed and nothing happened.

After two weeks with no clues, Joyce and Donald Hebert were at a loss. They had run out of options and were losing hope. Psychics across the nation had heard of the case and offered their services and, at this point, the Hebert family were willing to try anything. Several psychics gave vague hints that anyone could have come up with. Irene Hughes, a psychic from Chicago, told them Stephanie was south or southwest of her home and less than four miles away. Another, Dorothy Allison, who had claimed to have helped the FBI locate Patty Hearst, told the family that Stephanie would be found in a wooded area near a large body of water. Yet another, Charles Commander, claimed that he received telepathic visions and messages that a man was torturing the young girl.

———

Almost six months had passed and the trail had gone cold despite a $5,000 reward for information on the case. There were no more sightings of the heavily made-up woman or the Pontiac Trans Am. Although investigators still believed Stephanie had been kidnapped, it obviously wasn't for a ransom and they were fearing the worst.

———

In late November, twenty miles from the Hebert home, two hunters came across the skeleton of a young girl propped up against a fallen log in the woods. A long piece of rope draped across the bones, having once held tight against her skin. Less than five feet away, investigators found light blue eyeglasses, rubber flip-flops, and pink clothing.

Stephanie had chipped her front tooth a few months before she went missing. Her parents, however, didn't get the tooth fixed because it was a baby tooth and would have fallen out soon, anyway. Medical examiners matched the chipped tooth and determined it was the body of Stephanie Hebert.

There were no bullet holes in her skull or other signs of trauma that would determine exactly how she had died, but it was clear that she hadn't wandered into the woods on her own. Detectives were unsure whether she had been tied to the tree while she was still alive or if she had been killed first. There was no way to tell. Investigators scoured the area and used metal detectors to search for clues, but nothing besides Stephanie's belongings were found.

The FBI shipped her remains to Washington DC and the Smithsonian Institution analyzed her body, looking for a possible cause of death. However, there was so little of her left that they were unable to declare a definitive result.

––––––

Within a year of her death, prosecutors had come up with a theory. The night before she disappeared, Stephanie had gone to her friend Lorie's house for a sleepover and Lorie's brother, sixteen-year-old Roger Alexander, had been present. It's unclear, however, why they believed that Roger was involved. Although he had been at the home the night of the sleepover, he had a solid alibi for the entire following day; he was at a cousin's home nowhere near the Floral Acres subdivision and had witnesses to prove it.

Despite passing a polygraph, prosecutors brought the case to a grand jury. Any evidence against him, however, was entirely circumstantial and the grand jury refused to indict the boy.

––––––

For the next twenty years, Joyce and Donald Hebert were haunted by the murder of their daughter. Many people, including detectives that had worked the case originally, still believed that Roger Alexander may have been the killer. Although he had since moved out of state, suspicion followed Roger around for most of his life.

In 2006, Joyce Hebert reached out to a retired detective to help with the case. Although Major Sam Zinna hadn't worked the case originally, he agreed to look through old files and do his best to find her killer.

Zinna worked with the Jefferson Parish Sheriff's Office and was allowed access to the original case files and evidence, which included the rope that was found wrapped around Stephanie Hebert's skeleton. Zinna requested that the crime lab analyze the rope with modern technology that hadn't been available in 1978. After twenty-eight years, a partial DNA sample was retrieved from the rope that was believed to have been handled by the killer. However, it wasn't a match to the only suspect, Roger Alexander, and the case once again went cold.

————

In 2012, Tina Lewis had a secret that was eating her up inside. She was now forty years old and had held it in for most of her life, but she had finally built up the courage to tell someone. On July 24, she called the Jefferson Parish Sheriff's Office from her home in Arkansas and reported that she had been raped more than thirty years ago near her home in the Floral Acres subdivision in Waggaman.

Tina explained that when she was seven or eight years old, her family lived next door to a man named Daniel Parks. Parks had been a trusted friend of her father and had often babysat her and her younger brother. Tina wasn't sure of the exact date or even the year that it had happened because it had been more than thirty years prior.

She explained that one day she was playing at the Parks home with her brother and Parks' son when Daniel Parks asked the children to play hide and seek. Parks told his son and Tina's brother to go into the back bedroom and count to 100. When the two boys were gone, Parks took Tina by the hand and led her into the bathroom. Once inside, he closed and locked the door and turned off the lights.

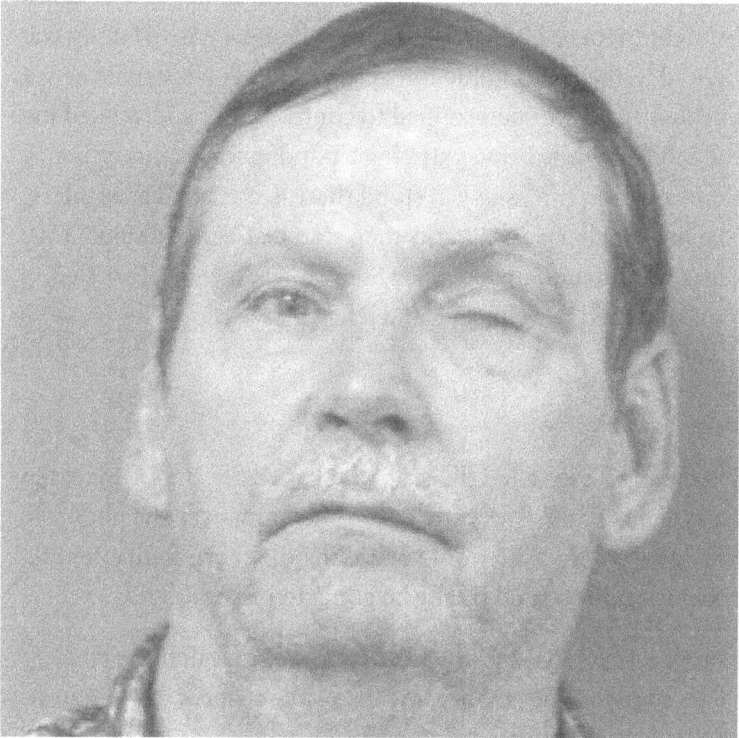

Daniel Parks

When Tina asked why the lights were out, Parks said, "So they won't find us." Parks then laid Tina on the bathroom floor and removed her shorts and underwear. Tina told investigators that she could still remember the sound that his zipper made when he unzipped his pants. He then laid on top of her and raped her. When Tina whimpered to Parks that he was hurting her, he muttered, "Don't worry, I'm almost done."

The two boys were knocking on the bathroom door when he got up, put his hand over her mouth, and whispered, "If you tell anyone about this, I'll kill your dad and your brother. Now get dressed and go play." Tina never told a soul.

Years later, in her twenties, Tina had children of her own and brought them to her parent's house when the entire family was invited to the Parks home for a crawfish boil. Now that she was an adult, Tina was determined to confront him and walked into the kitchen while he was stirring a pot of gumbo. But rather than confront him, she just stood there, frozen and speechless. She had lost her nerve. Parks then stared at her and said, "You don't want to end up like poor Stephanie, do you?" Terrified, Tina gathered her children and left.

———

Just before Tina called the Jefferson Parish Sheriff's Office, she had called Daniel Parks and confronted him over the phone. She told him that she would be calling the sheriff and after all these years, he would finally be going to prison.

On August 17, 2012, Daniel Parks Sr. was arrested. He was charged with rape and became the prime suspect in the murder of Stephanie Hebert.

———

During questioning, Parks initially denied raping Tina. He claimed that when the lights went out that day, he may have fallen on top of her but nothing had happened. As the interview progressed, however, he admitted that he might have touched her inappropriately.

Later in the day, Parks was questioned a second time. This time, he admitted that he had raped Tina.

"I hit the floor and my hand was in the right spot to feel something and I guess, you know, the animal instinct more or less started to take over."

He claimed that he was wearing short cut-off shorts and when he touched her, he was aroused and his penis "popped out." He told detectives that his penis made contact with her vagina but he pulled back quickly, claiming that the head of his penis touched her skin and penetrated her only one-eighth to one-quarter of an inch. But the amount of penetration was irrelevant. Either way, it was rape.

Later that night, in a third recorded interview, Parks recalled making the statement to Tina years later, telling her, "Get out of here before they find you like they found poor little Stephanie Hebert." But Parks denied having anything to do with Stephanie's disappearance or murder. He claimed that he only blurted that out to scare her, that it wasn't really a threat.

————

Daniel Parks was charged and tried for aggravated rape of a juvenile in December 2012. Another girl from the neighborhood that lived near both Tina and Stephanie testified on Parks' behalf, telling the court that she had spent the night at the Parks home several times as a child and had never encountered any inappropriate conduct from Parks.

His wife of forty-one years testified as well, saying that he had never acted inappropriately around children and they had never had complaints from anyone with children. Parks took the stand in his own defense and recanted his confession. He claimed that he hadn't eaten during his nine hours of interrogation. As a diabetic, he became lightheaded and said whatever he thought would get the interview over quickest.

His defense attorney pointed out that there was no physical evidence linking him to the crime and no proof that the crime had even happened. They argued that Tina couldn't even recall what year it had happened and accused her of having a "false memory."

Twelve jurors unanimously found Daniel Parks guilty of the rape of a juvenile. He was sentenced to life in prison without parole, probation, or a suspended sentence.

———

There was still the question of whether Parks had killed Stephanie Hebert. Although he was the prime suspect because of the comment he made to Tina, there was no physical evidence linking him to the crime. Furthermore, the partial DNA from the rope found around Stephanie didn't match his DNA. With no way to charge Parks, the murder case went cold for a third time.

———

Forty years had passed since Stephanie's murder and forty-seven-year-old Tom Martin couldn't hold his secret any longer. He had followed the story of his former neighbor, Tina Lewis, and admired how brave she was for finally having the courage to come forward after so many years. Tom, too, had a similar story that he was ready tell.

In November 2018, Tom Martin contacted the Jefferson Parish Sheriff's Office with a story very similar to Tina's. He, too, was sexually abused as a child when he lived in Floral Acres. Between the ages of two and six years old, Tom had been repeatedly molested by a neighbor – but it wasn't Daniel Parks. It was a man named Jason Vendrick Franklin. Not only had the man molested him, but Tom knew that Franklin had been molesting two other children in the neighborhood as well, one of which was Stephanie Hebert. At the time of her disappearance, Franklin had lived just eight houses away from the Hebert home on Aster Lane.

When the Sheriff's Office contacted the other living victim, forty-eight-year-old Diana Foster, she also told the story of her repeated rapes.

Detectives searched for Franklin and found that he had moved away from Louisiana sometime after Stephanie's disappearance. In 2011, he had been accused of taking obscene photos of a nine-year-old boy and was convicted of possession of child pornography.

On November 29, 2018, on the forty year anniversary of the discovery of Stephanie Hebert's body, seventy-two-year-old Jason Vendrick Franklin was arrested at his home in Pittsfield, Massachusetts, and brought back to Louisiana. At his home, investigators found huge collections of child pornography.

———

In March 2019, Franklin was indicted on three counts of aggravated rape of a victim under the age of thirteen: Tom Martin, Diana Foster, and Stephanie Hebert.

Jason Vendrick Franklin

Jason Vendrick Franklin became the prime suspect in Stephanie Hebert's death, although he had not yet been booked for the crime. Detectives announced that they had compelling evidence that Franklin was the killer, presumably the DNA from the rope found at the crime scene. Murder charges were inevitable but, with Franklin already in custody, prosecutors took their time building a solid case.

Franklin sat in the Jefferson Parish Correctional Center for the next two years awaiting trial for the rapes and knowing an impeding murder charge was coming. But in 2021, due to an undisclosed illness, he was placed into hospice care. He died in early 2022 without ever facing judgment for the crimes.

CHAPTER 3
THE EAGLE SCOUT

Like many other thirteen-year-old boys in the early 80s, Danny Joe Eberle's life revolved around his BMX bike. He spent hours thumbing through bicycle magazines, dreaming of the new parts he could buy for his shiny chrome bike. Danny and his family lived just south of Omaha in Bellevue, Nebraska, and his bicycle was the sole reason he delivered papers for the Omaha World-Herald.

Bright and early on Sunday, September 18, 1983, Danny Joe picked up his bundle of the Sunday Sunrise Edition of the paper at the Kwik Stop convenience store near his house. He spoke briefly to his supervisor Ray Rowell, rolled his newspapers, and then rode his bike toward the first house on his route.

Danny had left the Kwik Stop just after 5:30 that morning, but by 8:30 Ray Rowell received a phone call. Someone on Danny Joe's route had not received their paper yet. Danny Joe's route had only seventy houses; he should have been finished by now. Ray thought it was strange and assumed that Danny Joe had run late for some reason or had inadvertently missed a house on the route. However, just minutes later, another customer called.

Ray Rowell drove toward the first home on Danny Joe's route to see what was going on. The first three houses on the route had received their newspapers – but propped next to a fence in the front yard of the fourth house was Danny Joe's shiny BMX bicycle. Lying next to it was his bag of undelivered newspapers.

Danny Joe's bicycle was his pride and joy. It was everything to him, he never would have abandoned it. Ray Rowell immediately called Danny Joe's father, Leonard Eberle, but Danny wasn't at home either. Danny Joe's father and two brothers scoured the neighborhood looking for him, but he had simply vanished. Leonard then called the local police and an extensive search was initiated.

Right away, police suspected that Danny Joe had been abducted. Just thirteen days earlier another young boy, twelve-year-old Johnny Gosch, had disappeared two hours away in Des Moines, Iowa. Like Danny Joe, Johnny had disappeared while delivering newspapers. Johnny's newspapers and the wagon he carried them in were found at the first house on his route. Because of the similarities of the cases, the FBI was brought in to assist the Bellevue police.

The owner of the fourth house on Danny's route told police that he had noticed the papers and bicycle in the front yard around 6:30 that morning, when he left for church. Two hours later, when he returned from church, they were both still lying on the sidewalk. The man had moved the newspapers and bicycle inside his yard so they wouldn't be stolen.

More than 100 law officers from twenty-two different agencies all over Sarpy County were assisted by thirty representatives from nearby Offutt Air Force Base in the search for Danny Joe. The search was concentrated around nine square miles near the Missouri River, but after three days of searching there was still no sign of him.

That Tuesday afternoon, an eleven-year-old girl who was also delivering copies of the Omaha World-Herald reported that a man pulled up beside her in a car and motioned for her to come over. She refused, but the man insisted and motioned again. Frightened, the girl dropped her bicycle and newspapers and ran to the nearest house, where the homeowner called 911. The girl, however, wasn't able to provide a good description of the man.

On the Wednesday after he disappeared, the body of Danny Joe Eberle was found among tall weeds in a field along a remote gravel road just four miles south of his newspaper route. The body was less than twenty feet from the roadway and only two miles from Offutt Air Force Base. He laid face-down with his hands and feet tied behind his back. Although he was found wearing only his underwear, it didn't appear that he had been sexually abused. Surgical tape had been used to tape his mouth shut. He had died from nine stab wounds, with a gaping wound on the nape of his neck. An eleven-inch wide cut spanned the full length of his thigh and the flesh had been cut away to expose the bone. The lack of blood anywhere in the field told investigators that Danny Joe had been killed somewhere else and the killer had dumped his body in the field after his death.

In addition to the stab wounds, a spot on his left calf had been sliced several times, creating a star-shaped pattern. The slices suggested that Danny Joe had been tortured before his death. However, after closer examination, investigators realized the cuts were also an attempt to hide a clue: beneath the star-shaped pattern, investigators found a human bite mark.

The rope that was used to bind Danny Joe, at first glance, seemed to be ordinary nylon rope – but the inner core of the rope was unique. Inside the white nylon were 106 strands of yarn in twenty-four different colors. Each color represented a different type of fiber: acrylics, wools, cottons, rayons, nylons, and polyethylene. The FBI and the National Cordage Institute had never seen anything like it.

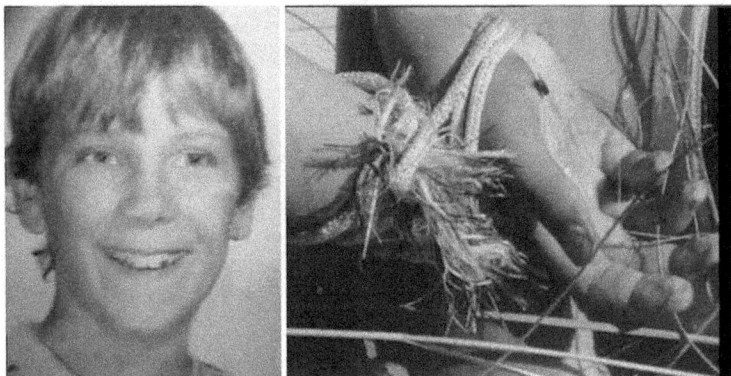

Danny Joe Eberle / Distinctive rope binding his hands

Just a week after the body was found, police arrested eighteen-year-old Michael Rice on unrelated charges of kidnapping, sexual assault, and making terroristic threats. The charges were linked to the molestation of two teenage boys from Nebraska. After his arrest, Rice had given a false alibi and later failed a polygraph test. However, he was ultimately released due to a lack of evidence. The FBI had also determined that he wasn't a suspect in the death of Danny Joe, as he didn't fit their profile.

———

On the morning of Friday December 2, 1983, twelve-year-old Christopher Paul Walden put on his red winter coat, slung his backpack over his shoulder, and headed out the door toward his sixth-grade schoolroom.

It wasn't until late that afternoon, when Christopher hadn't returned home from school, that his mother realized something was wrong. She was panic stricken when she called his friends, who told her that Christopher hadn't shown up for school that day.

Christopher's parents reached out to the media and issued an emotional plea for the safe return of their only child. Hundreds of volunteers helped in the search for Christopher.

Two days after his disappearance, two pheasant hunters found the body of Christopher Walden in a grove of trees five miles from the town. Two sets of footprints in the snow entered the grove, but only one set of footprints walked out. Like Danny Joe Eberle, Christopher was found face down. He laid in the snow and his throat had been slashed so deeply that it had nearly decapitated him. He had been stabbed to death. The full length of his chest and abdomen had been carved with cuts that resembled a large plant, with seven leaves and a stem. The slices also resembled the star pattern that was found on Danny Joe Eberle's chest. Christopher, however, had not been bound and appeared to have been killed shortly after he was abducted.

———

A witness came forward and claimed that she had seen Christopher walking to school that morning when a tan vehicle had pulled up next to the boy. She believed the man may have shown him something in his hand, but she wasn't entirely sure.

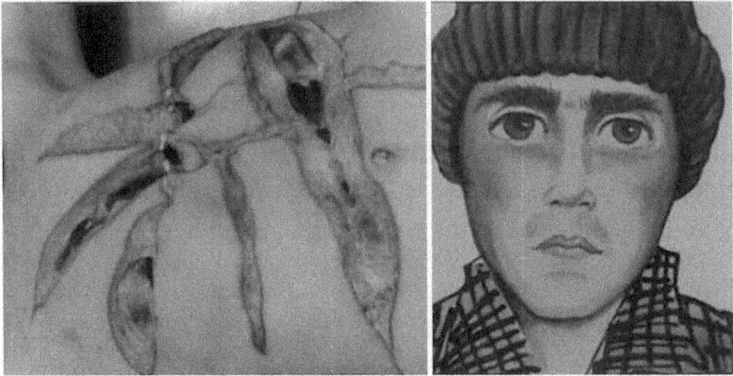

Carving on skin / Composite drawing of suspect

One of the officers working the case had been trained in hypnosis and believed that hypnotizing the witness may help her give a more accurate description of the man or the car. Although the hypnosis would not be useable in court, it could at least help find a suspect.

With the help of the hypnosis, investigators released a more accurate composite drawing and description of the car that the suspect was driving. The suspect was described as a white male with an olive complexion, eighteen to twenty-five years old, five-foot-eight to five-foot-ten, and weighing around 160 pounds. He was wearing a dark stocking cap, a plaid wool jacket, and gloves.

Investigators believed the car was a medium-sized late model sedan, cream colored, and with a light blue or faded dark blue interior. Police announced that they believed the suspect was responsible for the murders of both Danny Joe Ebele and Christopher Paul Walden.

Several leads came in with sightings of the suspect but each one was a dead end. In a televised press conference, the frustrated Sheriff of Sarpy county challenged the killer to turn himself in.

The terrified residents of eastern Nebraska and western Iowa were on edge.

———

Barbara Weaver had prayed daily for almost two months for the capture of the killer. On the morning of January 11, however, she said a special prayer. She prayed that the Lord would use her to help find the killer in some way. That morning, her prayer was answered.

Barbara worked as a preschool teacher at the Aldersgate United Methodist Church in Bellevue and had arrived early in the morning to prepare for her class. At 8:30 A.M., she noticed a car pull into the parking lot of the school. It was too early for parents to drop off their kids. The man slowly drove by the window of the classroom and stared in, but he then sped off when he noticed that Barbara was staring back at him.

The car returned a few minutes later. This time, the driver pulled up to the window and stared directly at her. Barbara was alone in the school and the man's stare made her uneasy. As the car left the parking lot a second time, she memorized the license number.

Just a few minutes later, the car returned a third time. The man parked and got out of the car. Barbara met him at the door of the school – the young man claimed he was lost and asked for directions. When he asked to use the telephone, however, Barbara still felt uneasy and directed him to a pay phone down the street.

The man then pushed her toward the school door, pulled a knife out of his pocket, and yelled, "Get in there or I'm going to kill you!" Barbara acted quickly and ran past him, toward the house of the church pastor who lived next door. When she got to the house, she pounded on the door and yelled, "Call the police! Call the police! That's the guy!"

By the time the police arrived, the man had driven away. The car he was driving wasn't tan, as the witness had reported seeing during the Christopher Walden abduction, but that didn't matter. Barbara had the license plate number.

Police ran the license plate number and tracked it to a rental agency that had rented the car to an enlisted radar technician from the nearby Offutt Air Force Base. When police entered the shop where twenty-year-old John Joubert worked, the entry door had a poster with the FBI composite sketch of the suspect. It's likely that Joubert and his co-workers saw the image every day as they went to work.

John Joubert was arrested and brought in for questioning, where he said very little other than that he had nothing to do with the killings. He was a highly decorated Eagle Scout – the highest ranking in the Boy Scouts of America – and volunteered as an assistant scoutmaster for the local troop. He had only recently joined the Air Force the year before, when he had moved from his hometown of Portland, Maine.

Although Joubert had rented the car, he owned a tan Chevy Nova that was in the shop being repaired. He matched the witness description perfectly. When police searched the Chevy Nova, they found a length of white nylon rope in the glove box. The inner core of the rope contained the same 106 unique colored strands of yarn. Joubert claimed he got the rope years earlier in the Boy Scouts, but the FBI discovered that the rope was extremely rare and had been produced in South Korea specifically for the U.S. military. More importantly, it was a perfect match for the type of rope used to bind Danny Joe Eberle.

Investigators also found a roll of brown packing tape and a knife in the car. Brown head hairs consistent with Danny Joe Eberle's were found on the car's carpet. In his dorm room, investigators found an assortment of porn and true crime magazines with similar stories of abduction and murder.

When FBI agents spoke to police in Joubert's hometown of Portland, Maine, they made a startling discovery: there had been a similar murder in Portland just one year prior. The murder occurred just before John Joubert joined the Air Force and moved to Nebraska.

———

On August 22, 1983, just before John Joubert moved to Nebraska, eleven-year-old Ricky Stetson had been jogging through Black Cove Trail near his home in the Oakdale neighborhood of Portland, Maine. When night had fallen and he hadn't returned home, Ricky's panic-stricken parents called the police. The next day, a motorist found Ricky's body alongside Interstate 295, which ran next to the park. He had been partially undressed but not sexually assaulted. He had been stabbed and strangled. Just like Danny Joe and Christopher, Ricky had been bitten and the bite mark had been sliced with a knife.

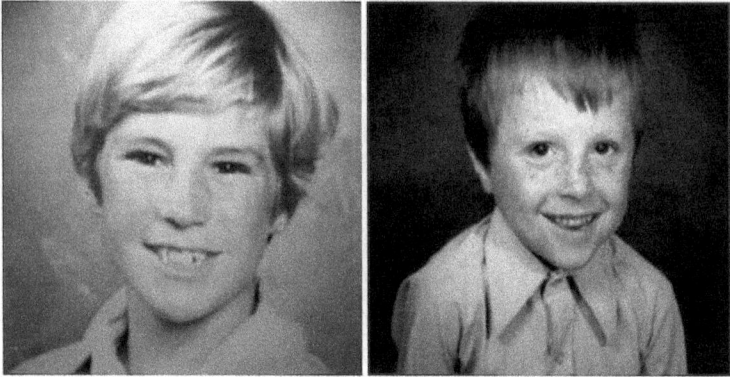

Christopher Walden / Ricky Stetson

A series of knifings had occurred in the same area in the weeks before Ricky's death and the police believed they were all related. The victims that survived described the attacker as a white male in his early twenties. However, the attacks miraculously stopped just after Ricky's murder. It was the same time that John Joubert had joined the Air Force and moved to Nebraska.

When confronted with the evidence against him, John Joubert admitted to killing Ricky Stetson in Portland. Then, just after moving to Nebraska, he killed Danny Joe Eberle and Christopher Walden. He also confessed to several stabbings in Portland dating back to when he was only sixteen. He claimed, however, that he had not killed Johnny Gosch in West Des Moines, Iowa, despite the strange similarities in the murders.

John Joubert

Joubert was fully aware that he was a monster and claimed that he felt relief when he had finally been apprehended. He told detectives that he unquestionably would have continued killing boys.

———

John Joubert was born into a working-class family in Lawrence, Massachusetts, on July 2, 1963. When his parents divorced, he and his mother moved to Portland, Maine. Joubert claimed to have had sadistic thoughts as early as six years old, when he fantasized about torturing, killing, and eating his teenage babysitter. By the time he was eight years old, he was obsessed with the idea of abducting, binding, torturing, and killing random strangers.

When he was thirteen, he put his dark fantasies into action and stabbed a nine-year-old girl with a pencil. The following day, he slashed another girl with a razor blade as she rode her bicycle past him. He later told psychologists that both incidents excited him sexually. At school, he was known as a bully who tormented children smaller than him.

Joubert excelled in the Boy Scouts, eventually earning the highest rank of Eagle Scout. He volunteered his time, played clarinet in the school band, and was an honor student with an IQ of 123. However, his sadistic fascinations overwhelmed him.

At sixteen, Joubert nearly killed two eight-year-old boys when he beat and strangled them before stealing their money. Throughout his later teens, he randomly stabbed boys younger than him and earned the name "The Oakdale Slasher." All the while, he went undetected by the police.

After high school, Joubert briefly attended Norwich University in Vermont. Although he had excelled in high school, he often skipped classes and failed after his first year of college. He later returned home to Portland.

Just after his twentieth birthday, Joubert attacked, strangled, stabbed, and bit eleven-year-old Ricky Stetson. It was his first kill. Worried that he might be caught, he joined the Air Force and continued his killings in Nebraska.

————

When asked if he disliked the boys — if that was why he killed them? — he replied, "How could I dislike them? I didn't even know them."

During his interrogation, John Joubert gave investigators information that hadn't been released to the press – information that only the killer would have known. He told them that he had stopped at a convenience store to get something to drink in the early morning of September 18. While he leaned against his Chevy Nova sipping his drink, he watched Danny Joe Eberle rolling newspapers in front of the store. It was still dark as the boy rode his bicycle toward his route and Joubert followed.

Joubert passed Danny Joe and parked a few blocks ahead of him in an empty parking lot. He grabbed a knife, a length of rope, and some tape, then hid behind a tree waiting for him to ride by. As Danny Joe walked back to his bicycle after delivering a paper, Joubert attacked, putting his hand over his mouth and the knife to his throat.

Joubert warned him not to make a sound and walked him to his parked car. He told Danny Joe to lie down on his stomach next to the car, where Joubert tied his hands behind his back and his feet at the ankles. He then put tape on his mouth, picked him up, and put him in the trunk.

Joubert drove erratically to a rural road south of the town and carried Danny Joe twenty feet into a cornfield on the side of the road. He then untied him and told him to remove his clothes. The tape covering Danny Joe's mouth had come off and he pleaded, "Please don't kill me." That was when Joubert stabbed him in the back.

Danny Joe begged, "Just take me to the hospital. I'm bleeding! I won't tell anyone!" But Joubert just stabbed him again. And again. He then sliced him deep into the back of his neck, killing him. Joubert continued to bite, cut, and slice. In all, Danny Joe had been stabbed eleven times. He also suffered damage to the top of his skull from being thrown around in Joubert's trunk.

After the murder, Joubert stopped at a McDonald's where he washed the blood from his hands in the bathroom and ordered breakfast. He then went back to his barracks and napped.

During the interrogation, Joubert also told the story of the killing of Christopher Walden. He explained that on the morning of December 2, he took the same knife he had used to kill Danny Joe and left his barracks at around 6:00 A.M. He drove from bus stop to bus stop looking for someone – anyone

– to kill. That was when he saw Christopher Walden walking to school.

Again, Joubert drove ahead of him, parked, exited his car, and waited for him to walk by. When Christopher walked past his car, he called to him, "Hey kid. Come here." He showed him the knife. "Keep quiet and come with me or I'm going to kill you." He then put his hand on Christopher's shoulder and steered him toward the car.

Joubert opened the door and told him to crawl in and lie down on the floor on the passenger side. When twelve-year-old Christopher began to cry, Joubert considered letting the boy go. He only gave it a second of thought before he reconsidered.

Again, he drove to a secluded road away from prying eyes and parked the car near some railroad tracks. He ordered Christopher out of the car and walked him through the snow down the tracks, reassuring him along the way that if he just did as he was told, everything would be okay.

When they reached a clearing, Joubert ordered the boy to strip down to his underwear and lie on his back. Christopher scoffed, "Huh? It's cold and there's snow on the ground." Joubert grabbed the boy's shoulders, shoved him to the ground, and yelled, "Do it!"

Once on the ground, Joubert straddled the boy, wrapped his fingers around his neck, and strangled him. Christopher fought to get away, but Joubert grabbed the knife and stabbed him several times and sliced his throat. He continued stabbing even after he was sure that the boy was dead. He then drove back to his barracks and threw the knife in the garbage. Later that day, he attended a Boy Scout meeting where they discussed the news of Danny Joe Eberle and Christopher Walden.

———

John Joubert was charged with the murders of Christopher Walden and Danny Joe Eberle on January 12, 1984. Initially he pleaded not guilty but later changed his plea to guilty. Psychiatrists diagnosed him with schizoid personality disorder, obsessive-compulsive disorder, and suicidal tendencies. However, they also determined he was not psychotic at the time of the murders.

A panel of three Nebraska judges sentenced Joubert to death for the two murders. In Maine, bite marks on Ricky Stetson were matched to Joubert. He was found guilty and sentenced to life in prison for the murder.

In prison, Joubert studied law, read Albert Camus and Sigmund Freud, and pleaded for his life to be saved. He claimed to have become a changed man, having finally fallen in love for the first time with a woman in Ireland who had written to him. However, he wavered back and forth from claiming to be reformed, to stating that if he were ever to be released, he would kill again. He said the need to kill was ingrained in him.

Ultimately, his pleas for leniency fell on deaf ears and John Joubert was put to death in an electric chair on July 17, 1996. Some people still believe that Joubert was responsible for the death of Johnny Gosch, but no definitive evidence exists to support that theory. To this day, the death of Johnny Gosch remains unsolved.

CHAPTER 4
BABY LOLLIPOPS

On the morning of November 2, 1990, a Florida Power & Light crew was working on an electrical box along North Bay Road, where it met with 58th Street in Miami. The street was known for its multi-million dollar beachfront homes hidden from the streets behind lavish private gates.

Along the base of one of the home's exterior walls, tucked behind a clump of palm trees and a cherry hedge, one of the workers noticed what seemed to be a piece of garbage. Maybe a lollipop candy wrapper. When the man looked behind the foliage, however, he stumbled back in horror. He realized it wasn't a wrapper but an emblem on a tiny shirt. On the shirt was a lollipop decal. The shirt was worn by a baby boy.

The boy appeared to be around two years old. It was hard to tell. His wavy brown hair was matted to his brown, emaciated skin, which draped over his bones like wet paper. His arms were thin and bony and his right eye was severely bruised. One leg was swollen to twice the size of the other from extensive beating. On his chest was a t-shirt adorned with three lollipops. His dark blue shorts covered a swollen diaper filled with excrement that had been sealed to his skin with duct tape. It had hardened like a cast and hadn't been changed in a very long time.

The medical examiner determined that the boy had died of blunt force trauma – his skull had been fractured. The blow that killed him had severed spinal nerves at his brain stem. The massive head injury may have occurred days or hours before his death.

The boy had suffered the most severe of abuse. He had been burned with cigarettes, several bones were broken, and his front two teeth had been broken out more than a year prior to his death. The tissue between his lips and gums was gone. Bedsores covered his body as if he had been bound to a bed for days at a time, maybe longer. He had been beaten badly and starved. He was anemic, malnourished, and dehydrated. One of his arms had been broken and the untreated scarred muscle had transformed into bone, permanently fusing his arm at a ninety-degree angle. The excrement from the duct tape-fixed diaper had caused a severe infection at the tip of his penis that would have made urination intensely painful. From the amount of bruising and scaring, it appeared that the boy had suffered unimaginable abuse for several months before his death.

The medical examiner estimated that the boy was around two years old, but he weighed only eighteen pounds. Half of what a boy that age should weigh. Investigators checked databases of known missing children, but the description matched nothing.

As police searched for clues near where the boy was found, a four-year-old girl and her mother stood near the police tape. The lead detective on the case was speaking to the woman and mentioned that they couldn't bury the baby without a name. Until they found out who he was, they would need to give him a name. The little girl looked up at the detective and said, "I can help." The officer asked the girl, "What name would you give him?" The young girl had heard that the baby had a shirt with lollipops on it and replied, "I'd call him Baby Lollipops."

Initially, the story of the abandoned boy wasn't front-page news. On November 4, only a few paragraphs were buried on page five in the B section of the Miami Herald. However, the media coverage was enough to grab the attention of a young woman who had worked as a babysitter. The woman came to police on November 6 and said that she may have an idea who the boy was.

The young woman told police that she had babysat for a woman named Anna Maria Cardona two years ago. Twenty-one-year-old Anna Maria had dropped off two of her children, the youngest of which was one-year-old Lazaro Figueroa. But Cardona never returned to pick up her children. Three months later, the babysitter handed the children over to the Florida Department of Health and Rehabilitative Services (HRS).

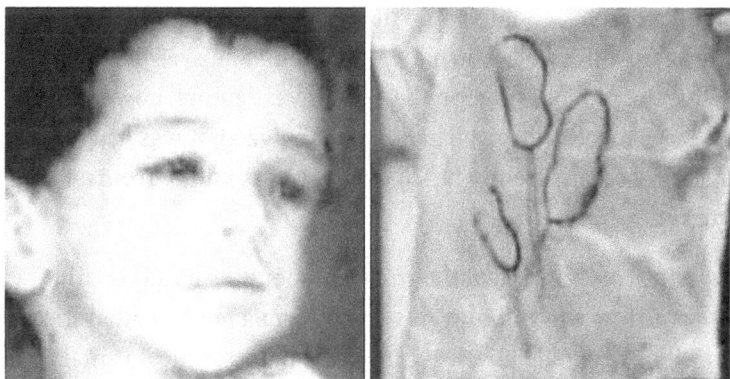

Lazaro Figueroa / Lollipop shirt

The children stayed in the custody of HRS for three months until they tracked down Cardona. The children were returned to the custody of their mother under state supervision. The state ordered Anna Maria to allow access for social workers to

check in on the family and required her to attend family counseling and drug abuse therapy. Unfortunately, immediately after
the children were returned to her, Anna Maria disappeared
with the children. Two years later, the emaciated boy matching
Lazaro Figueroa's description was found dead beneath a cherry
hedge. However, detectives still needed to confirm that the boy
was indeed Lazaro.

Over time, the media covered the story in depth and the hunt
for Anna Maria Cardona was aired on America's Most Wanted.
The news caught the eye of a fourteen-year-old mentally
disabled girl who also claimed to have babysat Lazaro Figueroa.
She told detectives that she was instructed to feed the boy
oatmeal and water twice a day, but sometimes forgot to feed
him at all. She said the boy cried constantly, that he was not
circumcised and she claimed to have taped his diaper on – facts
that had not been released to the public.

The girl then confessed to killing the boy. She said that one
night, when he wouldn't stop his incessant crying, she threw the
boy against the wall. The blow killed him. She even showed the
police the reddish stain on the wall. Investigators, however, cut
the large piece of drywall and had it analyzed. It was ketchup.
The girl had apparently heard details of the killing from an HRS
worker.

Investigators continued their search, spending a full month
after the boy was found trying to confirm a positive identification. The original babysitter knew the name of the hospital
where he was born, but the hospital claimed that Anna Maria
Cardona had given birth to a girl. They later came back and
realized they had made a mistake: the birth was indeed male.

Then, when detectives asked if the boy was circumcised, they
said that he was. The boy found in the bushes, however, was
not. The hospital again came back later and said they had made

another mistake. While Anna Maria Cardona had made an appointment for circumcision, she didn't show up. After a month, investigators were finally able to locate Anna Maria Cardona and positively identify Lazaro Figueroa's body.

————

Fidel Figueroa was known as Pepito on the streets of Miami in the late 80s. He was ostentatious and liked to show off his riches. He wore a diamond-studded Rolex, drove a new Mercedes, and traveled with several bodyguards. He kept two luxurious penthouse apartments overlooking the Biscayne Bay for his girlfriends but had many other women on the side.

Fidel Figueroa had immigrated to the United States in the early eighties and worked his way up to become one of the largest drug dealers on the streets of Miami. His life was a story that mirrored that of Al Pacino in Scarface – that is, until the evening of September 20, 1987, when he was shot in the head as he left a riverfront bar.

Four weeks later his son, Lazaro Figueroa, was born to Anna Maria Cardona, one of the women Fidel kept a penthouse apartment for. Fidel left Anna Maria $100,000 in his will – an amount of money which, in the late eighties, could have lasted a decade for some people. For Anna Maria, it lasted only a few months. Anna had begun a relationship with Olivia Gonzalez, who she met in a Miami night club, and the two of them quickly spent the money on massive cocaine parties. When the money was gone, Anna Maria abandoned her two youngest children with the babysitter.

————

Anna Maria Cardona had immigrated to the United States from Cuba during the Mariel boatlift in 1980, where 125,000 Cubans arrived by boat to Florida. In Cuba, she had been raised by an abusive single mother and was sexually assaulted at the age of ten. She began drinking, doing drugs, and selling sex on the streets of Havana in her teenage years and had attempted suicide several times. When she arrived in the United States in the early eighties, she immediately turned to a life of crime, doing anything she could to survive. She was arrested three times in 1982 and 1983 for breaking into homes.

All that changed, however, when she met Fidel Figueroa. She quickly became accustomed to a lavish lifestyle of fine jewelry and fancy cars which all came to an end when Fidel was gunned down. Cardona sank into an uncontrollable cocaine addiction. Just as quickly as she had come up from the streets, she was back on them. This time she had three children with her.

Immediately after HRS handed the children back to their mother, she was gone and HRS had lost track of the family. The case worker waited a full four months before informing the judge handling the case that the family was missing. By that time, there was no way to find her and the case fell through the cracks.

———

One month after Lazaro Figueroa's body was found, detectives tracked down Anna Maria Cardona and her girlfriend, Olivia Gonzalez, in St. Cloud, Florida, near Orlando. They brought the pair of them back to Miami for interrogation.

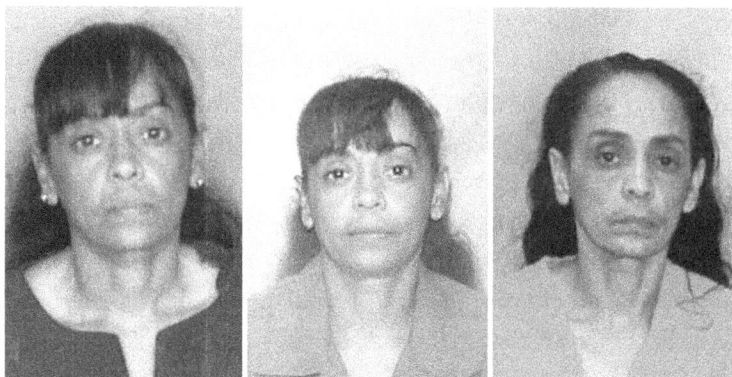

Anna Maria Cardona

Anna Maria Cardona couldn't keep her story straight. Initially, she claimed that she'd left the boy with a babysitter and that was the last she had seen of him. She then said she gave the boy to an "elegant woman" who had approached her in a cafe. She quickly changed her story and said that Lazaro's death had been an accident: she and her son had been jumping on the bed when he fell off and cracked his skull. Finally, she admitted that she and Olivia Gonzalez had beaten the boy and told detectives that Lazaro was still alive when she left him in the bushes. In court, she blamed the abuse on her lover, Olivia Gonzalez. She claimed that she chose the affluent neighborhood of mansions because she thought he would have a better chance of living a full life if he was found alive there.

———

For eighteen months after she gained control of her children again, Anna Maria Cardona and Olivia Gonzalez systematically tortured Lazaro to death. She blamed him for her descent "from riches to rags."

Lazaro spent much of the last year and a half of his life tied to a bed, locked in a closet, or left in a bathtub with cold or hot water running. If he complained in the slightest, he was beaten or choked. All the while, his mother and Olivia Gonzalez consumed whatever drugs they could get their hands on. They moved between cheap hotels and rented rooms often and survived by shoplifting and occasionally taking odd jobs. For those eighteen months, the only people that ever saw Lazaro were his older brother and sister, twelve-year-old Juan Puente and five-year-old Taimy Cardona.

———

Both Anna Maria Cardona and Olivia Gonzalez were charged with aggravated child abuse and first-degree murder. The two were then quick to blame each other for the killing.

Olivia Gonzalez accepted a deal and pleaded guilty to second-degree murder in exchange for a lighter sentence. She also agreed to testify against Cardona. While she admitted that she had played a role in the murder of Lazaro, Gonzalez claimed the majority of the abuse was carried out by Cardona. Gonzalez was sentenced to forty years in prison but served only seventeen.

At the first trial of Anna Maria Cardona, Olivia Gonzalez provided graphic testimony of the last moments of Lazaro's life. She told the court that on Halloween night, 1992, Cardona was angry with her son, picked up a baseball bat, and hit him over the head. "A hole opened up in his head. His head was cracked. It was bleeding and bleeding and bleeding. Then I put mercury on it and applied a plastic band." She then said that Cardona had strangled the boy because he wouldn't stop crying before she put him back in the closet.

Gonzalez claimed that Cardona's cocaine use was actually a good thing. She said that when Cardona was high on cocaine, she didn't abuse her son as much. She told the jury that Cardona had once given Lazaro cocaine and sprayed him with insecticide just for a laugh. Gonzalez claimed that she was afraid to stop her because Cardona could get violent when confronted, once having stabbed her in the hand.

Cardona, however, placed the blame squarely on Gonzalez. She claimed that she had been forced into a sexual relationship with Gonzalez in exchange for food and shelter. She admitted that she had been addicted to crack cocaine at the time and let the abuse happen, but she also insisted her son would still be alive if it weren't for Gonzalez. Ultimately, the jury didn't buy her story. The abuse had happened over a very long period and there were many witnesses that testified to her abuse. Cardona was found guilty of first-degree murder and was sentenced to death.

Ten years later, however, Cardona's conviction was overturned. Her defense attorneys had not been given access to Gonzalez's police interviews, some of which contradicted her testimony. In her original interrogation, Gonzalez had told investigators that she was the one that had hit Lazaro with the bat, cracking his head open.

The second trial of Anna Maria Cardona began eighteen years after the murder. Her defense team, however, was grasping at straws: this time they tried to lay blame on the fourteen-year-old mentally disabled girl that had confessed to killing Lazaro. Of course, there was no evidence to back up their defense and Cardona was found guilty again. She was sentenced to death a second time.

Cardona's defense team appealed once again and, in 2017, the second conviction was overturned. This time it was because the prosecution had "improperly inflamed the minds and passions of the jurors" by repeatedly calling for "Justice for Lazaro" during closing arguments.

Anna Maria Cardona was fifty-six years old during her third trial in December 2017. This time, the prosecution didn't seek the death penalty. Her defense again focused on the fact that Gonzalez had confessed to hitting Lazaro with the baseball bat – but, again, jurors heard from friends and acquaintances who testified that Cardona had often treated her son badly. Her lawyer told the court that while Cardona was indeed a bad mother, she wasn't a murderer. For a third time, however, the jury didn't agree.

Anna Maria Cardona was once again found guilty of murdering her son, Lazaro Figueroa. As Judge Miguel de la O sentenced her to life in prison, he told her:

"I don't think you will be meeting Lazaro in the afterlife. Your actions were monstrous. My mind recoils at the hellish existence you put Lazaro through that last year of his life. There are wild beasts that show more empathy to their offspring than you showed to Lazaro."

Cardona played the victim and screamed back at him in Spanish,

"I didn't kill my son! I didn't torture my son! Maybe you don't believe me. Maybe you don't feel my pain. Nobody could love my child more than me!"

———

Lazaro's older brother, Juan Puente, had spent his entire adult life in and out of prison. His mother's reputation followed him throughout his life. He had been convicted for robbery, grand

theft, battery, burglary, cocaine possession, disorderly intoxica-
tion, prowling, and loitering. Eventually, he was labeled a
habitual violent offender. During the sentencing of her second
conviction, he was brought from a Miami jail to plead for his
mother's life. Juan Puente died in prison at the age of thirty-
seven, just two months after his mother's third conviction.

CHAPTER 5
PIED PIPER OF TUCSON

Charles "Smitty" Schmid made up for his five-foot-three stature by filling his cowboy boots with newspapers and crushed beer cans. It gave him an extra three inches of height, but it also gave him a ridiculous limp that he explained away by telling friends that he got it while fighting members of the Mafia.

Schmid was odd on many levels, but somehow the young girls of Tucson, Arizona, in the late 1950s and early 60s were drawn to him. He was naturally good-looking with a slight resemblance to Elvis Presley – and he went to extremes to amplify that likeness. He wore pancake makeup on his face, dyed his reddish-brown hair black, and drew a fake mole on his cheek. The mole started as a small dot and, over time, grew to the size of a dime. He even used a clothespin on his lower lip in an attempt to make it droop like Elvis'. He wore so much lip balm – incessantly so – that his lips took on a thick, white sheen.

Charles wanted to look tough and would often tape a metal bridge to his nose, claiming it had been broken in a fight. He regularly kept a toothpick in his mouth which he constantly wiggled back and forth as he spoke. He carried small shakers of salt and pepper with him everywhere he went and told his friends that he would use them to blind his opponents. Schmid often claimed to have psychic powers that allowed to him to see events before they happened.

———

Charles Howard Schmid Jr. was born in 1942 to an unwed couple in Tucson, Arizona, who put him up for adoption. The following day he was adopted by Charles and Katherine Schmid, who owned and operated the Hillcrest Nursing Home. His mother raised him to be extremely polite, well mannered, and not care what others thought of him.

During his childhood, Schmid was intelligent but had no interest in school. As a result, his grades were barely above failing. What he lacked in education, though, he made up for in sports. In 1960, he led the high school team to the Arizona State Gymnastic Championship.

Although Charles didn't get along well with his father, his parents thought the world of their only son and pampered him. When he turned sixteen, his parents let him move into a detached home at the back of their property, where he could live on his own. His mother still cooked his meals and paid all of his bills, but he was allowed to come and go as he liked. They purchased a new car and motorcycle for the young boy and provided him with a $300 monthly allowance. The equivalent of about $2,700 today.

Despite his abilities in gymnastics, Schmid quit the team during his senior year. This was around This was around the same time same time that he was told he was adopted. When Charles tracked down his birth mother, she wanted nothing to do with him. She told him to leave and never come back.

Just before his high school graduation, Schmid was caught stealing tools from the school's machine shop and was temporarily suspended. After his suspension, however, he didn't return to school. Instead, he chose to live off of his ample allowance.

Schmid's eccentricities and the fact that he had a car, motorcycle, and his own home gave him a cult-hero status among the other teenagers of Tucson. He had no problem dating girls and often dated several at a time. Young boys admired him and wanted to emulate him. Schmid became the charismatic ringleader of the teens that hung out on Speedway Avenue, the main drag that ran through Tucson. He held large parties at his home and his parents didn't seem to mind. Schmid did whatever he wanted to do, whenever he wanted to do it – and every kid in town envied him.

He and his friends spent their nights drinking while they cruised up and down Speedway Avenue. Although some of his closest friends and been convicted of robberies and petty crimes, Schmid had been lucky. He'd had only a few run-ins with the law but, so far, it had been nothing major.

In 1963, Schmid started dating an eighteen-year-old high school dropout named Mary French. Mary had a cold exterior and was unpopular with the other teenagers in the Speedway crowd, but she and Schmid were in love. When he lied to his parents and told them that they had eloped, they allowed her to move in with him and gave her a job in their nursing home. The money she earned, however, went straight to Charles.

On May 30, 1964, Charles confided to Mary that he had always wanted to kill someone. He knew he could get away with it. It didn't really matter who – he just wanted to see what it felt like. He gave Mary a list of three girls and told her to choose one for him to kill. Mary chose her fifteen-year-old neighbor, Alleen

Rowe, a sophomore at Palo Verde High School who lived with her divorced mother. Alleen wasn't one of the trouble-making crowd that hung around Speedway Boulevard. She was a good kid that got good grades and had a promising future. In fact, she was Mary French's opposite. Maybe that was why she chose her as Schmid's first victim.

The next day, Charles Schmid enlisted the help of his close friend, John Saunders. Mary spent the day convincing Alleen Rowe to sneak out with the three of them on the night of May 31 to a party in the desert. It would be a double date.

Alleen reluctantly agreed and waited until after her mother left for work at 11:00 P.M. that night. She snuck out of the house, still wearing curlers in her hair.

The four drove into the desert and parked on a remote road in the foothills of north Tucson – a favorite place of Schmid's that he had often taken girls to drink and have sex. The four of them walked into the desert, to a dry creek bed where they could sit and drink. Knowing what was about to happen, Mary said she was going to go back to the car to listen to the radio for a bit.

As Mary sat in the car, she wasn't listening to the radio. Instead, she sat in the dark and listened to Alleen's screams echo through the quiet desert. The two men had tied her hands behind her back, removed her dress, and laid it on the ground. They laid her on top of her dress and Schmid instructed Saunders to rape her, but he couldn't do it. He would rather just kiss her, but it felt strange to kiss her while she was crying.

Schmid, frustrated with his friend, told Saunders to take a walk in the desert and come back in a few minutes. When Schmid called for Saunders to come back, Alleen was crying and putting her dress back on. She started walking away from her assailants into the desert.

The two men followed her and Schmid handed a large rock to Saunders. Saunders told him, "I can't do it," and walked back toward the car. Minutes later, when Saunders returned with Mary, Alleen was laying on the ground with a pool of blood around her head. Schmid was laughing and excited. His hands and shirt covered with blood.

In the bright desert moonlight, Schmid, Saunders, and French spent the rest of the night digging a hole to bury Aileen. Her curlers, which they noticed later, had fallen from her head. They were buried in a separate, shallow hole nearby.

———

Alleen's mother, Norma Rowe, worked the night shift as a nurse. When she arrived home the following morning to find her daughter's empty bed, she panicked. She called all of Alleen's friends but none had heard from her. She could sense that something was wrong and reported her daughter missing. Alleen had recently told her mother about sex clubs at her school where kids were involved in prostitution, alcohol, and drugs. The officers that took her statement, however, thought she was crazy. They had never heard of such a thing at Palo Verde High School.

Police did, however, question everyone that knew Alleen, including Schmid, Saunders, and French. All three had conspired ahead to repeat the same story. They claimed that they had stopped by Alleen's home that night but she hadn't answered the door, so they went out on their own.

In the days after her disappearance, Alleen's father had dreams of his daughter. He dreamed she had been murdered in the desert. The dreams were so real, they had to mean something. He begged the police to search the desert surrounding Tucson, but detectives insisted they would need more evidence than just a dream to justify a search like that. Besides, the desert around Tucson was enormous. They wouldn't even know where to begin.

Norma Rowe spent the next year diligently contacting the Arizona Attorney General, the FBI, reporters, and even a psychic. However, at every turn she was told that Alleen was probably just upset that her parents had divorced and had simply run away from home.

———

The impact of the murder had driven a wedge between Charles Schmid and Mary French. Gradually they saw less and less of each other. A few months after the murder, John Saunders joined the Navy and left Tucson. With John gone, Schmid started hanging around a new friend, Richie Bruns.

Bruns had a reputation among the teens of Speedway Boulevard as a creepy guy that was awkward around girls. There had also been rumors of Bruns being involved in the murder of an older man. The rumor was that man had befriended Bruns and showed him his revolver. The man then propositioned him for sex. Richie was shocked and turned down the man's advance. Days later, the man turned up dead and Richie's fingerprints were all over the gun that had killed him. For a time, Richie Bruns was the main murder suspect, until another man from Phoenix was eventually convicted of the murder. The case, however, had put Bruns on Tucson Police's radar.

Like many other Tucson kids, Bruns looked up to Schmid because of his peculiar style and his way with women. Gradually Schmid and Richie became the best of friends and Schmid let him know of his dark secret: the murder of Alleen Rowe.

In July 1964, Schmid started dating a young, blonde, seventeen-year-old named Gretchen Fritz. Gretchen was the oldest daughter of a well-known heart surgeon in the Tucson area. Although Gretchen came from an affluent family, she was rebellious and odd, to the point that her teachers claimed she was psychotic. Like Schmid, she was known for doing whatever she wanted, whenever she wanted to do it. For Schmid, it was a match made in heaven. He was in love.

Almost immediately, Charles and Gretchen's relationship was fraught with jealousy. He was still fooling around with Mary French and several other girls on the side – and Gretchen knew it. It infuriated her. It didn't help matters that Gretchen and Richie didn't get along, either. Richie Bruns was socially awkward and didn't get along with almost any girls, but he particularly hated Gretchen. The feeling was mutual.

Not long after they began dating, Gretchen heard rumors that Charles had once asked Mary French to marry him. The thought of it threw Gretchen over the edge. Not only had Charles Schmid given Mary an engagement ring, but he had also given another girl a ring.

At one of the frequent parties at Charles's home, Mary French approached him and claimed she was pregnant with his baby. The next thing he knew, Gretchen claimed she was pregnant as well and wanted Charles to marry her. Schmid did his best to calm both girls for the time being.

Charles Schmid like to brag and eventually it had become common knowledge among the Speedway teens that he had murdered Alleen Rowe. Most of the teens, including Gretchen, had heard the rumor. However most weren't quite convinced that it was true.

In early August 1965, however, Gretchen made a discovery while rummaging through Charles's home, looking for evidence of his love affairs. She found his diary. The diary, of course, detailed the rape and murder of Alleen Rowe.

When Gretchen confronted Schmid about the diary, he admitted that he had killed Alleen Rowe. In fact, he also claimed to have killed a sixteen-year-old boy years earlier, cutting off his hands and burying him in the desert.

The news that her boyfriend was a murderer didn't seem to bother Gretchen, though. In fact, she didn't see it as bad news at all. She saw it as an opportunity. Leverage. Gretchen informed Schmid that he would need to stop seeing any other girls immediately, or she would tell the police that he'd killed Alleen Rowe. And with the diary, she had the proof in his own handwriting. But Charles Schmid wasn't about to be blackmailed.

On the evening of August 16, 1965, Gretchen and her thirteen-year-old sister, Wendy, drove Gretchen's red and white Pontiac Le Mans to the Cactus Drive-In to see *Tickle Me* starring Elvis Presley.

Alleen Rowe / Gretchen Fritz / Wendy Fritz

During the movie, Gretchen had learned that Charles Schmid was having a party afterward. But there was no party and after the movie Gretchen and Wendy didn't return home. While it wasn't unusual for Gretchen to stay out all night, Wendy was another story. Wendy was young and trustworthy, the opposite of her older sister. Their worried father searched for the girls, then later called the police to report them missing.

Two days after they had gone missing, police received a report that the girls may have been hitchhiking south of Tucson. A couple had reported picking up two girls matching their description along the highway and had driven them to Nogales, Arizona, where they may have crossed the border into Mexico. The couple believed the girls were Gretchen and Wendy.

Four days after the girls had gone missing, a private detective hired by the girls' father found Gretchen's car parked at the Flamingo Hotel in Tucson. The keys were still in the car, as was Gretchen's purse. Both the front and back seats had traces of mud on the floor. Witnesses had seen the girls at the drive-in, but no one had seen them park the car at the hotel.

Range Deputies were sent to Mexico to look for the girls. One week later, they heard reports that the girls had been seen on the beach in Mazatlán. Ultimately, detectives were unable to confirm any of the sightings. After being missing for several months, the police gave up and determined that the two girls had simply run away.

Everyone that Gretchen and Wendy had associated with was interviewed by detectives, including Schmid and Bruns. During questioning, Bruns had no problem admitting to detectives that he disliked Gretchen. In fact, he hated her. Still, he insisted he knew nothing about the girl's disappearance.

When detectives interviewed Schmid, he told them he believed the girls had run away to San Diego. Gretchen and her family had vacationed in San Diego just a month before the disappearance. Schmid explained that when Gretchen returned from vacation, she had bragged to all her friends of a summer love affair she had with a young man in San Diego.

———

Several months had gone by with no sign of Gretchen, Wendy, or Alleen. Bruns and Schmid were drinking at Schmid's home one evening when Schmid confided, "Well, I suppose you know what happened to Gretchen?" Bruns had assumed she was in San Diego, just like Schmid had told him, but then Schmid told him the truth.

Schmid claimed that he had killed both girls right there in his home, strangling them with a guitar string. At first Bruns didn't believe him, just as he didn't believe the story that he had killed Alleen Rowe. But Schmid said he could prove it.

Schmid drove Bruns into the foothills north of Tucson, far into the desert. There, among the sagebrush, were the bodies of

Gretchen and Wendy Fritz. They were so badly decomposed that Bruns hardly recognized them as bodies. That night, Bruns helped Schmid dig graves in the desert to bury the girls.

———

That November, Bruns was arrested for disorderly conduct. He was sentenced to six months of probation, but he would have to spend the probation time in Ohio, with his grandmother, instead of Tucson. Bruns hated being forced back to Ohio. He had finally begun dating a girl named Darlene Kirk in Tucson, but he wouldn't be able to see her for six months.

Bruns sat at his grandmother's home and stewed. Now that he knew that Charles Schmid really was a killer, the thought occurred to him that his girlfriend, Darlene, could be his next victim. Worried that Schmid may continue his killings, Bruns called Tucson police.

Bruns told detectives that if they could get him back to Tucson, he would tell them who killed Gretchen and Wendy. He would even take them to the bodies. Detectives made a deal with Bruns and agreed that he wouldn't be charged for the crimes, then returned Bruns to Tucson.

Bruns took detectives into an area in the desert off Pontatoc Road, where they unearthed the skeletal remains of the two Fritz girls. Strewn throughout the desert near the graves, they found fragments of clothing, a small shoe, and a clump of blonde hair.

———

On November 10, 1965, Charles "Smitty" Schmid was arrested and charged with two counts of murder. One was for the Fritz sisters and the other for Alleen Rowe, even though they didn't have Alleen's body. Bruns didn't know where Alleen was buried.

Detectives brought Mary French and John Saunders in for questioning and offered them deals. For their testimony against Schmid, they would receive reduced sentences. Both took the deal. However, when French and Saunders took investigators into the desert where they had buried Alleen Rowe, all they found were her hair curlers. The body had been moved.

The murder case attracted major publicity. Time, Life, and Playboy Magazine all sent reporters to Tucson to cover the case. The magazines dubbed him The Pied Piper of Tucson because of his cult-like status among the young people of Tucson. The publicity attracted the attention of a man living in the Phoenix area who claimed he could find things in the desert using a divining rod, a forked device that was typically used to find water or minerals in the desert. The man searched the area and found a spot where he believed the body of Aileen was located. However, when the police dug they found nothing.

Mary French pleaded guilty to being an accessory to murder and was sentenced to four to five years in prison. Saunders pleaded guilty to second-degree murder but was given a life sentence when he later changed his mind and refused to testify against Schmid.

———

The prosecution had a problem, though. Their case revolved around the assumption that the motive for killing Gretchen and Wendy was because Gretchen had threatened to tell the police of the murder of Alleen Rowe. But without a body, there was no proof that Alleen Rowe was even dead. They were desperate to have the trial of the murder of Alleen happen first. Unfortunately, they didn't get their wish.

The trial for the Fritz sisters began in February 1966, giving an advantage to Schmid and his defense team. It didn't matter. The jury convicted him on both murder charges and Charles Schmid was given a death sentence for each.

The trial for the murder of Alleen Rowe began in May 1967. Schmid's mother hired celebrity defense attorney, F. Lee Bailey, to consult with his defense attorney. Bailey had become famous for working for the defenses of Albert DeSalvo, Sam Shepard, and Patty Hearst.

During the last days of the trial, the court was adjourned for a short recess. When they returned, Schmid's lawyer announced that he had changed his plea. Schmid asked to change his plea to guilty of second-degree murder; the prosecution accepted. A few days later, however, Schmid filed a motion to fire his attorneys and withdraw his guilty plea. The judge denied his request and sentenced him to fifty years to life for the murder of Alleen Rowe.

About a month after starting his sentence, Schmid asked to speak to the Pima County Sheriff. He finally wanted to show where he had buried the body of Alleen Rowe. He insisted that he hadn't beaten her over the head and said that, once the body was found, they would see that her skull wasn't fractured.

In handcuffs, Schmid was driven from the prison into the desert north of Tucson. The body of Alleen Rowe was found just twenty yards from where the man with the divining rod had indicated. Her skull was indeed fractured.

Three years after his convictions, the state of Arizona temporarily abolished the death penalty and his sentences were commuted to fifty years to life.

During his incarceration, Schmid attempted to escape several times, once using a hollow gymnastics horse and another time faking suicide. One escape attempt, in November 1972, was successful. He escaped with Raymond Hudgens, another inmate who had had also murdered three people. The two fugitives held four people hostage on a ranch in Tempe, Arizona, before they were recaptured three days later.

In 1974, Charles Schmid officially changed his name to Paul David Ashley. It's unclear why. The following year, he was attacked by two other prisoners and stabbed twenty times in the face and chest. He died ten days later from the injuries on March 30, 1975.

CHAPTER 6
THE SLUMBER PARTY

Twelve-year-old Jessica Thornsberry was the middle sister of three. Her sisters, Stephanie and Patricia, were just a year younger and a year older than her. All three girls attended Southern Middle School in Louisville, Kentucky, and were active in the Cloverleaf Baptist Church.

As young girls often do, the three loved to spend the night at friends' houses, where they could stay up late and gossip about school and boys. Jessica usually stayed at the home of April Gipson, who lived just a few houses down the street. April was also twelve and she and Jessica were the best of friends.

On the evening of March 29, 1995, Jessica's mother, Diana Thornsberry, dropped her off for a sleepover at April Gipson's house at around 8:00 P.M. But as soon as her mother arrived back home, Jessica called. She wanted to double-check to make sure it was okay for April's mother, Carolyn Gipson, to dye her hair. Diana told her daughter it was fine and the two girls walked to the store to buy some hair dye.

On their way to the store, the girls walked with two young boys from the neighborhood. After they returned, Carolyn dyed

Jessica's hair and all three of them watched television while April's seventeen-year-old brother, Jeremy, and his girlfriend were in an upstairs bedroom.

Late that night, April and her mother fell asleep in the living room but Jessica was wide awake. She watched television by herself in the kitchen.

Around 11:00 P.M., April heard a knock on the front door and woke up from her position on the living room floor. She noticed that Jessica had opened the front door. Moments later, Jessica whispered to April that the boys from earlier in the evening were back and wanted to hang out. April was too tired and told Jessica to make them go away. Instead, Jessica went outside with the boys. April had no idea that this would be the last time she would see Jessica alive.

———

The next morning, when Carolyn Gipson woke to go to work, she saw her daughter, April, still sleeping on the floor, but Jessica was gone. She assumed that the living room floor may have been too hard for Jessica and she had gone upstairs to sleep in April's bed.

April awoke shortly after her mother left for work and went looking for Jessica. She wasn't upstairs and she wasn't outside of the house. Assuming Jessica had awoken early and went back home, she called Jessica's mother. Jessica wasn't at home and Diana Thornsberry knew something was wrong. She immediately reported her daughter missing and went out looking for her.

At 8:15 that morning, county workers were untangling some straw netting on a drainage project in Iroquois Park just four miles from the Gipson home when they found a tiny female body. The body had been loosely wound in the straw netting and placed between the golf clubhouse and the riding stables.

The workers frantically flagged down a police officer that had been in the park. Sergeant Yates slowly unwrapped the body from the straw. Once he saw her green sweatshirt and black jeans, he knew it was the body of Jessica Thornsberry.

Diana Thornsberry had only reported her daughter missing an hour earlier and her body had already been found. From the ligature marks around her neck, it was obvious she had been strangled. When police broke the news to Jessica's family, her younger sister, Patricia, fell to the floor in tears while her older sister, Stephanie, ran from the home screaming.

Right away, detectives interviewed those who had last seen her, including the two young boys that had shown up at the house after 11:00 P.M. Investigators soon realized, however, that the two boys, aged eleven and thirteen, had nothing to do with Jessica's murder.

April and Carolyn Gipson were interviewed as well, but they were baffled as to who would have done such a horrific thing. April's older brother, Jeremy, told detectives that he had seen April on the phone at around 11:30 that night, but that was the last time he saw her. However, when detectives interviewed the next-door neighbor, Mike Moberly, the pieces started to fall into place.

Twenty-five-year-old Mike Moberly lived just a few feet away from the Gipson home and the two homes shared a common driveway. Moberly told police that he was awoken by a noise outside of his window at 3:30 A.M. He had heard someone walking between their homes. When he looked outside, he saw a blue Chrysler LeBaron in the driveway. The car belonged to Rachel Theiss, the girlfriend of Jeremy Gipson. Seventeen-year-old Jeremy was standing beside the car, smoking a cigarette.

Thinking nothing of it, Moberly went back to bed. But ten minutes later, he couldn't sleep and glanced out of his window again. This time, he noticed that the car had been moved. It was now backed into the driveway with the trunk facing the Gipson home. Still, he assumed it was nothing out of the ordinary and Moberly went back to sleep.

When police asked if he believed Jeremy may have been involved, Moberly shunned the idea. He told detectives that he and Jeremy had been playing basketball in the driveway just the afternoon before. "He's a good guy. He couldn't be involved." He added, "Although, I heard he had some problems with the police a few years ago, but I'm not sure what it was about."

Detectives were more than curious at what kind of prior "problems with the police" Moberly was referring to. When they looked up the juvenile record of Jeremy Gipson, they were speechless. Two years earlier, when Gipson was just fifteen years old, he admitted to the rape of a seven-year-old girl. Unbelievably, the offense had been "informaled," meaning the charges were dropped in exchange for the offender promising to do something. In Jeremy's case, the charges were dropped with the promise that he would go through counseling. Jeremy Gipson, however, only attended a few of the counseling sessions and never showed up again. The prosecutors handling the case failed to bring him back to court when he didn't live up to his end of the bargain and the case fell through the cracks. Jeremy had raped an innocent young girl and gone completely unpunished for the crime.

To make matters worse, Kentucky juvenile cases were (and still are) protected by secrecy laws – laws that were designed to protect the offender rather than the victim. Diana Thornsberry had no way of knowing that when she agreed to let her daughters stay the night at the Gipson home, as she often did, they weren't safe. They were under the same roof as a child predator, which ultimately led to Jessica's demise.

With this new knowledge, investigators questioned Jeremy Gipson once again. This time, Jeremy asked that his mother not be in the room for the interview. Then he had a different story to tell.

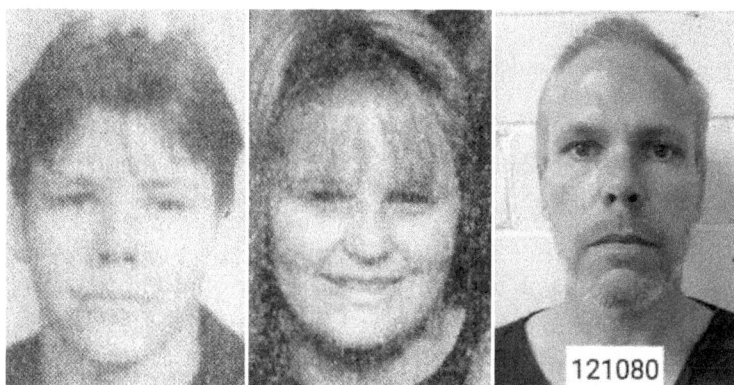

Jermey Gipson & Jessica Thornsberry

Jeremy told detectives that he had left the Gipson home late that night and hung out with two older men, although he didn't know their names. The three of them were drinking alcohol, smoking marijuana, taking methamphetamines, and drinking something he was told was "liquid acid" or LSD.

When he arrived back home in the early morning hours, his girlfriend, Rachel, was asleep in an upstairs bedroom and he went into the basement to smoke more marijuana. That was when, according to Jeremy, Jessica came down the basement stairs. Apparently, Jessica had a crush on Jeremy and had for quite some time. In fact, he claimed she was even mad at him because he was dating another girl.

Jeremy told investigators that Jessica had smoked a joint with him. When he asked her to help him find his marijuana pipe and she refused, he hit her in the back of the head. In a drug stupor, he struck her over and over again, then wrapped his hands around her neck and started choking. Jeremy pulled down her pants and raped her while he tightened and released his grip on her neck over and over again. He then rolled her over and sodomized her while still choking her. By the time he had finished, he realized she was dead.

In a feeble attempt to make it seem as if Jessica had committed suicide, he grabbed an electrical cord, wrapped it around her neck, and pulled. Gipson realized, however, that the suicide of a happy twelve-year-old wasn't going to seem believable. He then put her in the trunk of his girlfriend's car, wrapped her in straw netting that he found, and dumped her body in Iroquois Park.

Sixty-two days after he murdered Jessica Thornsberry, Jeremy Gipson was arraigned, pleaded guilty, and sentenced to life in prison with the possibility for parole in twenty-five years. In February 2020, Jeremy Gipson was denied parole. He will be eligible for parole again in 2030.

CHAPTER 7
BEYOND REDEMPTION

Just northeast of downtown Philadelphia, Pennsylvania, along the Delaware River, Fishtown had been a working-class neighborhood for centuries. However, an era of deindustrialization in the 1980s and 1990s caused many of the "rust belt" cities in the United States to drop into poverty, when families that had worked in heavy industry and manufacturing lost their jobs.

Although Fishtown today is a thriving neighborhood with hip coffee shops and expensive loft-style apartments, it was a rough place for a kid to grow up in the early 2000s.

Sixteen-year-old Jason Sweeney, however, wasn't your average kid. He had ambition and knew exactly what he wanted to do with his life. He wanted to be a Navy Seal – and he was well on his way. He had been accepted to Valley Forge Military Academy but didn't yet have the money to pay the school's tuition. Although he had dropped out of high school, he had a steady job working for his father's construction company and saved everything he earned to pay for his tuition.

———

Ever since the fourth grade, Jason had been best friends with his neighbor, Eddie Batzig. During their pre-teen years, Jason and Eddie had done everything together; played video games, listened to music, and everything else that typical young boys would do. When they were both fourteen, Jason went to the Jersey Shore with Eddie's family and, later that summer, Eddie went with Jason's family on vacation to Florida.

Eddie Batzig & Jason Sweeney / Jason Sweeney

But a few years later, just after Jason had dropped out of school and started working for his father, Eddie and Jason began drifting apart. Jason had tried to hold on to the friendship, but Eddie had become influenced by two other boys from the neighborhood, sixteen-year-old Nicholas Coia and seventeen-year-old Dominic Coia.

For a brief time, Jason was welcomed into the new clique of boys, but right away Jason noticed that the brothers were different. While Jason was doing his best to better his life, he could see that the Coia brothers were nothing like him. They had no plan for life other than doing drugs and causing trouble. Sadly, they had influenced Eddie to do the same. Eddie, Nicholas, and

Dominic grew jealous of Jason because he was earning money and saving for tuition, while they were just drifting aimlessly through life.

———

In late May 2003, over the Memorial Day weekend, Jason met a fifteen-year-old girl named Justina Morley. He was instantly smitten. He was excited. For the first time in his life, he had a girlfriend and thought he was in love. For the next few days, Jason told his family that he couldn't wait until they met Justina. He was sure they would love her, too. She was so sweet. But Jason didn't know the full story behind Justina.

Justina Morley had been expelled from public school during the eighth grade, then attended the eighth grade for a second time the following year at a private Catholic school in Fishtown. It hadn't been the first time that Justina had repeated a grade. Justina had started smoking marijuana when she was just ten years old. It wasn't long afterward that she started snorting cocaine, stealing prescription pills, and smoking marijuana laced with embalming fluid. Just a few years later, she started cutting her wrists and thighs with razor blades and threatening suicide. Her mother had her checked into Friends Hospital in Philadelphia but later removed her against the advice of hospital staff.

Jason Sweeney had no idea what he was getting himself into with Justina. He also didn't know that when he met her, she was having sex with both Eddie Batzig and Nicholas Coia in exchange for heroin.

———

On May 30, 2003, just four days after meeting her, Justina told Jason she was ready to have sex with him. They just needed to find a secluded place where they could be alone. To a sixteen-year-old boy, those were magical words and Jason was excited beyond belief. Justina suggested they walk out to The Trails, a wooded area on the north bank of the Delaware River beyond a dead-end street of old warehouses.

Late that afternoon, Jason and Justina walked deep into the woods where no one could see. When she found the perfect spot, Justina stopped, kissed him, and told him to take off his pants. Without wasting a second, he complied. Jason first took off his shoes and unzipped, but before he could pull down his pants, he heard swift footsteps behind him – followed by a hatchet to his face.

———

Jason's parents were worried sick when he didn't show up that night and wasn't answering his cell phone. It wasn't like him. Jason was a responsible boy and would never have stayed out all night without telling his parents. His sister had seen Jason earlier in the day with Justina Morley, but she didn't really know the girl and had no idea how to contact her. By nightfall, the family called the police to report Jason missing.

At 2:00 PM the following day, two young boys riding mountain bikes on The Trails found the body of Jason Sweeney. Although police knew Jason had been reported missing and the clothes seemed to match the description of what he was last seen wearing, authorities were initially unable to identify him. His head was so severely beaten that it was barely recognizable as human. It was just a mess of flesh, blood, and broken bones. The only bone on his head that hadn't been crushed was his left cheekbone. That evening, Jason's parents were only able to identify him by a fresh wound on his hand, where he had injured himself working construction the week before.

———

Police asked Jason's family for a list of his closest friends so they could begin questioning and looking for clues. Jason's sister mentioned to police that she had seen him earlier in the day with Justina Morley, but when police arrived at Justina's home, her mother said Justina hadn't been home for the past few days and she had no idea where she was. Police worried that whoever had killed Jason had abducted Justina, so when she turned up two days later, they were relieved. But Justina had a story to tell.

———

Detectives questioned Justina Morley, Eddie Batzig Jr., Nicholas Coia, and Domenic Coia simultaneously in four separate interrogation rooms so the detectives could bounce back and forth between the teens to verify their stories.

Justina told police that she and Jason went to The Trails to have sex when he was viciously attacked. When Jason heard the footsteps behind him and turned to see what was happening, he saw his best friend since fourth grade, Eddie Batzig, and the two Coia brothers. Eddie swung at him with the hatchet, landing blow after blow. Jason cried, "Please stop! I'm bleeding!" But Eddie didn't stop. When Jason tried to run, Nicholas Coia followed quickly after him with a hammer. Nicholas pounded his head repeatedly. Domenic Coia then grabbed large rocks and beat Jason on the head. Justina told police, "It was horrible. It seemed like forever."

Justina Morley / Domenic Coia / Nicholas Coia / Eddie Batzig

Justina blamed the brutal killing on the three boys, but when the boys were questioned, they told investigators that Justina was just as much a part of the murder as anyone else. Although she may not have struck Jason, she was an active participant in the planning of the killing and even lured him to The Trails for the specific purpose of killing him.

All three boys told the same story. Jason gushed blood and pled for his life while they continued the brutal assault. Domenic told detectives, "We just kept hitting and hitting him." Lying on the ground, barely able to see through the blood dripping into his eyes, Jason looked up at Justina and said, "You set me up." Those would be his last words. The final blow came from the older brother, Domenic Coia, who grabbed a large boulder and dropped it on his head.

All four teenagers knew that Jason had just cashed his check from his construction job and had $500 on him. They took the money, his wallet, and a pack of gum. Domenic Coia told detectives that as they walked away from the murder scene, they stopped for a group hug, laughed, and screamed. "Then we split up the money and we partied beyond redemption."

Investigators asked Domenic Coia if he was high at the time of the murder. He responded, "No, I was as sober as I am now. It's sick, isn't it?" When Eddie was asked why he took the pack of gum, he coldly replied, "It's not like he was gonna need it." The four freely admitted to the brutal killing and claimed their motive was for the $125 each that they took from Jason's wallet. They spent the money on marijuana, Xanax, and heroin, but there was clearly more to their motivation than just money. It was a relentless lust for blood.

The four teens explained that they had been planning the killing for weeks and listened to the Beatles' song "Helter Skelter" on repeat as they made their plans. It was the same song that Charles Manson claimed had inspired him and his followers during their 1969 killing spree. Morley, Batzig, and the Coia brothers had planned every detail of the murder, including the weapons each of them would use and who would get to strike the first blow.

———

All four teens had explained their part in the crime, but they were also all juveniles. If they were tried as juveniles, there was a chance they would be back on the streets by the time they were twenty-one. Prosecutors needed to have them tried as adults to make sure they were never allowed out of jail for the rest of their lives. The only way to ensure that would be through eyewitness testimony – and the only way to get eyewitness testimony would be to make a deal with one of them.

Although Justina Morley was equally culpable in the murder, she hadn't actually struck any blows. Prosecutors offered Justina a lesser sentence of third-degree murder in exchange for her testimony against her conspirators. She took the deal and was sentenced to seventeen and a half to thirty-five years in prison.

Eddie Batzig, Nicholas Coia, and Dominic Coia were each charged with first-degree murder, conspiracy, robbery, and possessing an instrument of crime. None of them seemed the slightest bit repentant.

———

As they all sat in jail, Justina Morley played the role of the innocent young girl that had been influenced by the delinquent boys. However, through letters they sent back and forth to each other, her true colors came through.

All three boys were tried together as adults in March 2004. On the first day of proceedings, the U.S. Supreme Court, in a separate case, ruled that defendants under the age of eighteen could not be executed. Domenic Coia was just fourteen days shy of his eighteenth birthday when Jason Sweeney was murdered. That meant that the death penalty was off the table for all of them.

During the trial, Justina Morley cried as she recalled how the boys had bludgeoned Jason Sweeney in front of her. However, the defense didn't go lightly on her and confronted her about her jailhouse letters, where she shunned any remorse for the killing. Morley wrote to Domenic Coia:

"I am guilty. But I still don't feel guilty for anything. I still enjoy my flashbacks. They give me comfort. I love them."

In additional letters, she wrote:

"You asked how much we would bleed if we were together. Literally constantly. I would enjoy the blood every day. Torturing these pathetic people. I want to make them suffer. PASSION FOR MURDER!"

"...I like the movies about Hannibal Lecter and always wanted to live off of human flesh.

If I get out, I'm getting fangs put in permanently. I remember like two years ago, I tried to sharpen my teeth with a metal file."

Justina Morley wrote several sexually explicit and violent letters to all three of her accomplices.

"So you say I'm manipulative, and yes, I believe I am in ways. I'm persuasively manipulative, and I think I'm pretty good at it, too. I enjoy dragging people along.

Tell me you don't enjoy these gullible humans. It's funny how easy it is to persuade them into lies.

I'm a cold-blooded fucking death-worshipping bitch who survives by feeding off the weak and lonely. I lure them and then I crush them."

Yet another letter to Domenic read:

"It would be hard to make myself cry – to make people think I was remorseful, or scared, or whichever. It's fun making people think and be confused."

In additional letters to Domenic, she stated that if they were ever released, she wanted to have his baby. She also suggested that, in the event they didn't get released, they should agree to a suicide pact.

"You need to have offsprings with me. I need you! I'm serious and you should take me seriously into bed with you. I love you!

I don't care what or whom you killed. I really would applaud if you killed a person."

Morley admitted that she'd had sex with Batzig and Nicholas Coia for heroin just before the murder and that she had stripped for the three boys in a prison van when they all were first arrested.

Eddie Batzig wrote to her, "You're a great person, awesome chick, and a beautiful girl – or should I say, woman."

Batzig's attorney did his best to prove that his client had been influenced by Morley rather than the other way around. During cross-examination, he asked Morley, "Don't you think that you have these guys under control?"

She replied, "No."

He continued, "Didn't you talk about each of them doing these different kinds of violent things and how it would thrill you?"

"Yes," she replied.

"You didn't feel like they all worshipped you?"

"No."

She cried when she was shown photos of Jason's battered head and Batzig's attorney continued confronting her about her letter, where she wrote about making herself cry. He accused her of doing just that during the trial.

Additional letters from Morley were read for the jury:

"Remember I said I had this great dream? Well, it was about me and I killed this lady in my room. I beat her with a two-by-four. And then I cut her open and took out all her organs, cut her head, took out her brain.

I stuffed her in my closet for three days and noticed blood dripping from the ceiling into my living room and on my carpet.

I went upstairs, took her body, put it in the trash bag full of clothes and stuck her in a dumpster. Of course, I ate her brains and organs.

Then I keep killing females and eating their insides."

In another letter, she recalled the Edward Norton movie American History X:

"I remember the first time I watched it, I had a smile on my face. More so when he fucking stomped on the guy's head. I want to do that to someone. I think… no, I know, it would be fun. I have fun just thinking about it."

Another letter to Nicholas Coia read:

"You said we couldn't have sex if you got life, and I say why not? I'll do it right in the visiting room with everyone watching. Or I could wear a really short skirt with no underwear and I'll do it like that.

If I get pregnant, I promise to keep it, but what is the name going to be? Give me a boy and girl name."

Nicholas replied:

"I was stupid when we were free. I should have made you my girl. I really do like you. Remember the first time we went out? I loved you so much I had to leave you, 'cause I was scared you would abandon me like my mom did. I love you."

A letter to Domenic Coia read:

"So, Dom, for the record, when are you going to give into my love for you? I'm trying to be patient, but I don't have it in me."

That same day, she mailed a letter to Eddie Batzig which said:

"I miss your punk ass. You know you miss me, too. Don't lie. You know what I miss most? Your sex."

Batzig replied:

"Honestly, I thought I was falling for you. It was not love yet, but almost. I liked you enough to do the unthinkable. This summer would have been great, but now prison. It's not as bad as TV, but it's not freedom. Love, Eddie."

———

In May 2005, all three boys were tried as adults and found guilty of first degree murder, conspiracy, robbery, and possession of an instrument of crime. For the murder charge, each received a sentence of life in prison without parole. They all received an additional twenty-two and a half to forty-five years for the remaining charges.

Both during the trial and at sentencing, the three boys displayed no remorse for the murder. During the sentencing hearing, Jason Sweeney's father addressed Domenic Coia:

"Look at me, Domenic. I know you think you have evil eyes, but mine are going to be staring back at you every night for the rest of your life."

Domenic coldly replied, "I never thought I had evil eyes. But other than that, I'm cool."

———

Justina Morley / Domenic Coia / Nicholas Coia / Eddie Batzig

While Domenic Coia, Nicholas Coia, and Eddie Batzig will spend the rest of their lives in prison for the murder, Justina

Morley was released from prison in 2020 at the age of thirty-two.

CHAPTER 8
RAT IN THE OVEN

For most of his life, James "Jimmy" Sheaffer had problems with money. The thirty-six-year-old limo driver had no control over the little bits of money that he earned. In fact, the opposite was true; the money controlled him. As far back as he could remember, Jimmy's paycheck had been spent before he even had the chance to touch it. It was a common problem for many people, but Jimmy had let his finances come to a boiling point.

Although they weren't married, Jimmy and his girlfriend of seventeen years had three kids together and shared a home in the quiet suburban town of Deltona, Florida, thirty miles north of Orlando. His girlfriend, however, had no idea how far Jimmy had let his financial situation get out of hand until April 2013, when the water at their home was turned off.

But water was the least of Jimmy's worries. People were after him. Bad people. For years, Jimmy had gambled his earnings away. When his earnings ran out, he borrowed from friends and family members. When friends and family stopped lending him money, he borrowed from payday loan shops, then from his bookies. It was only a matter of time until those people would want their money back.

He had overdrawn every bank account that he'd ever had and, inevitably, the banks closed his accounts. Understandably, this caused problems for Jimmy, especially when it came time to cash the $1,200 social security disability check that he received every month.

Jimmy Sheaffer

In order to keep his financial woes from his girlfriend, Jimmy made a pact with his close friend, Angela Stoldt, who lived across the street from him. He had known Angela for five years and she agreed to help him cash his social security checks.

In order to cash his social security checks, Jimmy changed the payee of his benefits into Angela's name and Angela opened a bank account in her own name. When Jimmy's checks arrived, Angela deposited the $1,200 into the account. The plan was for Jimmy to withdraw $1,100 with the debit card that she had given him, which would leave $100 per month for Angela – her payment for doing her friend a favor.

She should have known, however, that supplying Jimmy with his own debit card was a very bad idea. From the very first month the account was opened, Jimmy withdrew more than the agreed-upon amount, leaving Angela with an overdrawn account. The overdrawn amount went onto a line of credit that piled up each month.

The agreement had gone on for eighteen months, but each month Jimmy continued to withdraw more than was in the account. The debt – for which Angela was solely responsible – grew and grew. Angela had no way to pay for the debt that Jimmy Sheaffer had accrued. She also had her own financial issues and her own set of problems.

———

Forty-year-old Angela Stoldt was born in Bangkok, Thailand. Her father was in the Air Force and she and her older sister bounced around from base to base until her teenage years, when the family settled down in Deltona, Florida. During her early years, Angela had trouble making friends. Every time she made friends with other kids on the current Air Force base, it was time for the family to move again. As a result, she grew up feeling alienated. She felt like an outcast everywhere she went, never quite fitting in with the other kids.

Angela suffered from depression and anxiety throughout her life, for which she was given medication. She also took medication for her hypothyroidism.

During her freshman year in high school, she started dating a boy three years older than her. He was her first boyfriend. Within months, fifteen-year-old Angela dropped out of high school, moved in with him, and the two got married.

By the time she was twenty, Angela had divorced her first husband and married once again. Although she and her second husband had a son together in 1996, just three years later they, too, were divorced.

At twenty-five, Angela met and married her third husband. Her new husband made a good living. They bought a home together and Angela gave birth to their baby girl. Angela and her third husband stayed together for thirteen years, until he developed health issues and began directing his anger toward her. In 2011, her husband walked away from their relationship and children.

Angela was once again a single mother with no means of supporting herself other than her own Social Security checks. To make matters worse, her efforts to help her friend with his financial problems suddenly became her own financial obligations.

———

Just after 3:00 A.M. on April 4, 2013, Jimmy Sheaffer had finished his route at Blue Diamond Limousines and pulled into the parking lot of his employer to return the car. He had spent the past several hours driving his client to Tampa and back and was ready to relax. But maybe a drink first. Jimmy dropped the keys with his boss and walked out of the office, where he got into a waiting car, leaving his own car behind.

The next morning, Jimmy's girlfriend, Candy, was worried when she realized he hadn't come home that night. Assuming he had possibly stopped by his parent's home after work, she called them. But they hadn't heard from him either. Jimmy's father called the police to report him missing.

Investigators started looking for Jimmy by checking with his employer and found his car still parked in the lot. Although his boss had seen him get into a car that evening, he hadn't bothered to look at the car and had no idea who might have picked him up. His employer and fellow employees said that Jimmy was well liked and a popular driver. He had regular clients that often asked for him by name.

Next, detectives spoke to Jimmy's friends and family. His girlfriend confirmed that she hadn't been the one that picked him up from work that night and had no idea who it may have been. She had, however, recently received a text from him. His text message was vague and insinuated that people were looking for him and he needed to lie low for a while. Her cell phone also showed that Jimmy had tried to call but hung up before she could answer. When police spoke to his friends, they found that many of them had received similar texts from Jimmy, saying that he was hiding out until it was safe to come back home.

To investigators, it seemed that Jimmy Sheaffer had simply run away. Maybe he owed people money and would return later by his own accord.

Investigators spoke with his neighbors, one of whom was Angela Stoldt, who lived directly across the street. She had been standing at her sidewalk watching the commotion around the Sheaffer house.

Angela told investigators that she knew Jimmy well. They often drank together and their kids were of similar ages and played together. Angela claimed to have no idea where Jimmy might be, but admitted she knew of his financial problems and that he had outstanding debts to several people. She also mentioned that she was the payee on his disability checks because he couldn't get them cashed.

Investigators looked more closely into Jimmy's debts and found that he had been borrowing frantically for the past five years.

Every cent he got his hands on blew through his fingers quickly. He had managed to keep the secret from his girlfriend, but it was obvious that he was worried. His mortgage payments hadn't been paid in months and the bank was threatening foreclosure.

Several days went by before investigators went back to Angela Stoldt to question her again. She wasn't under suspicion but, from what they could tell, she was Jimmy's best friend. If he was hiding out, maybe she knew where he was but just wasn't telling.

Angela insisted she wasn't helping Jimmy hide. To prove herself, she showed detectives her cell phone, where Jimmy had texted her that he was being chased by people. To appease them further, Angela invited them into her home. Inside, police found one of the most unkempt homes they had ever seen: junk and trash were piled literally everywhere through the house, leaving only small walkways between rooms. Although the home was messy, there was no sign of Jimmy and no sign of foul play.

Despite the fact Angela wasn't a suspect in any crime, investigators still had the intuition that she knew more than she was letting on. Thus, they brought her into the police station for official questioning. Once inside the interrogation room, detectives thought it was odd that she donned dark sunglasses and took a more defensive tone. She still insisted she had no idea where Jimmy was but her story had changed. This time she admitted to having seen Jimmy on the morning of April 4, the day he went missing.

Angela claimed that she met Jimmy at the bank, where she had opened the account for him and he gave her $150 to pay for overdraft fees. She also told investigators that he had stopped by her house later that evening and they spoke on her porch. She said that Jimmy was nervous and people were after him. He asked once again to borrow money. Angela claimed that both times she saw him, he wasn't alone. There was someone else in a car waiting for him, but she had no idea who it was or what they looked like. She hadn't even noticed what kind of car they were driving.

Angela claimed that she told Jimmy the police were looking for him and he should just turn to them for help, but he refused. He claimed that the people that were looking for him were using the police to find him.

Hearing Angela's story, detectives started to wonder if they would eventually find Jimmy dead at the hands of someone to whom he owed money. Although her stories were odd, they had no suspicion of her doing anything other than helping him hide.

———

More than two weeks had passed since Jimmy Sheaffer's disappearance and the mysterious texts from Jimmy to his friends and family had stopped.

The case, however, took a drastic turn on the evening of April 21, when police received a phone call from Angela's sister, April Leach. April told police that Angela Stoldt was mentally unstable and threatening suicide.

When Angela spoke to police, she asked to speak to the lead investigator handling the Jimmy Sheaffer case. She was a mess when she arrived at the police station, crying hysterically and barely able to speak in full sentences. In preparation for the interrogation, the investigator read her Miranda rights and she got quiet. "I need to speak to an attorney," she said.

The investigator ended the interrogation before it began but, despite asking for an attorney, Angela kept talking. She muttered, "You guys should have stopped me. You could have ended it before it got to this point."

The investigator, however, was unable to continue the interrogation since she had asked for legal representation. Angela was transferred to a nearby mental health facility but only a few hours passed before she asked for the investigator once again. This time, she was ready to talk without an attorney.

"I want to tell you what happened to Jimmy," she said.

———

Angela told detectives that she was the one that had picked up Jimmy from the limo lot that night at 3:00 A.M.

They left his car there and drove to her house, where they drank vodka and peach schnapps and took Flexeril, a strong muscle relaxant that she had stolen from her father's medicine cabinet.

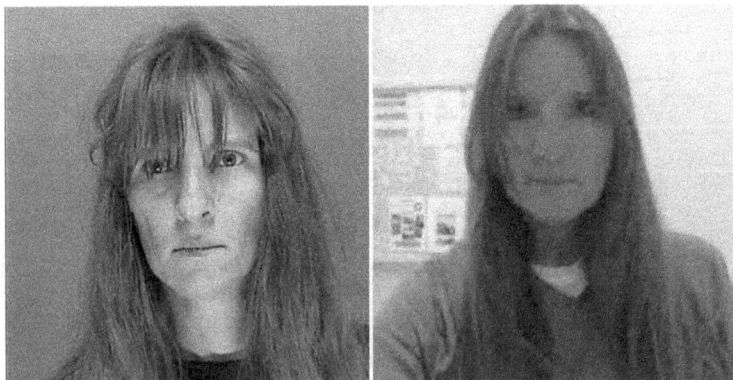

Angela Stoltd

Jimmy, of course, wanted to borrow money and asked Angela to speak to her father to see if he would loan him $4,000 to pay off some of his debts. Angela lied to Jimmy. She said she'd already spoken to her father and he would loan him the money, but Angela hadn't spoken to her father and had no intention of helping him. She had helped him far more than any other friend would have; he had returned the favor with lie after lie. She wanted him to feel what it was like to be lied to.

Angela claimed that, at 5:00 A.M., she drove him to the Osteen Cemetery and parked. They had often talked there before. Jimmy, however, believed that they were driving to her father's house. Once they parked, she told him that her father wasn't going to give him any money and neither was she.

Angela told Jimmy that she was taking the check cashing advance off of the bank account. That meant that if the balance was below zero, the bank would no longer issue credit. He wouldn't be able to withdraw until he paid the balance that was already outstanding.

Angela told detectives that Jimmy flew into a rage. He put his hands around her neck and tried to strangle her. Jimmy yelled, "I trusted you! I need that money! Our whole family is going to get kicked out. Don't you fucking care that my children are going to be homeless?"

Angela said she feared for her life and reached her arm into the back seat, looking for something to protect herself with. She put her hand inside a cardboard box full of camping gear on the back seat. She blindly fumbled around in the box until she felt a wooden handle. Then she pulled out an icepick and shoved it into Jimmy's eye.

Jimmy was still coming at her. Angela reached again into the box and pulled out a length of rope with plastic handles on each end. It was a tool used to climb trees. She wrapped the rope around his neck, pulled the handles, and strangled him to death in the front seat of her car.

After he was dead, she explained that she pulled the icepick out of his eye, wrapped his head in cling wrap, and propped him up in the seat. She stared at him for a few seconds, then shoved the icepick in his other eye and drove home.

When detectives asked where the body was, Angela cried, "I just thought that if I could reduce it down to size that I could make it disappear."

"How?" they asked.

"I had to cut him up."

———

Angela Stoldt explained how she drove Jimmy's body back to her home and dragged him into the garage. Using a hacksaw, she dismembered the body and placed the parts into two kiddie pools to contain the mess. Then, piece by piece, she cut the body into small, manageable chunks.

She told detectives that when they were questioning her on the sidewalk just after Jimmy went missing, she had his head in a pot on the stove, attempting to boil it down to nothing.

"If you would have walked just a little bit more towards my house, you would have smelled his body parts in the oven."

When Angela's daughter complained of the smell of burning flesh, she reassured her that it was just a rat that had snuck into the oven.

Angela butchered, boiled, and cooked Jimmy's body parts for days in her home. She told her son that it was parts of a deer that she had hit with her car.

After tightly sealing the remaining parts in black plastic garbage bags, she enlisted the help of her son to distribute them around the city in random dumpsters. She buried his cell phone in one location and his driver's license in another.

Angela explained how she used Jimmy's cell phone to send misleading texts and hang-up phone calls to his friends and family so they would assume he was running from those to whom he owed money.

When police searched the dumpsters in which she claimed to have dumped the body parts, they found nothing. At an illegal dump site near the Osteen Cemetery, however, investigators found some of Jimmy's clothes, the soup pot, a thigh bone, a kneecap, and chunks of flesh. They were the only pieces of his body ever found.

Angela showed no remorse and told detectives, "I'm sorry, but I put Jimmie where he belonged."

———

Angela Stoldt was charged with first degree murder, abuse of a dead body, and tampering with evidence. She admitted killing Jimmy Sheaffer, dismembering his body, and tampering with evidence but claimed it was all in self-defense. It was either kill or be killed. Despite her claims of self-defense, investigators found that she had purchased plastic wrap and rubber gloves at Walmart just hours before the murder.

———

Angela Stoldt's murder trial began in December 2014 and the prosecution's star witness against her was her own sister, April Leach. April told the court that two weeks after Jimmy was reported missing, Angela was having an emotional breakdown and called a "family meeting." At their parent's house, she told April and their parents that she had done "the most deplorable thing in the world."

But she told her family a different story than the one she told police. She claimed that there was no struggle between Jimmy and herself. She told her family that she had used the muscle relaxer to put Jimmy to sleep, then strangled him. She put the icepick in his eye afterward just to make sure he was dead.

Angela's defense attorney argued that her confession had been acquired after being admitted to a mental health facility and she hadn't slept in days.

Angela took the stand and explained that she killed him in self-defense, then only cut him up and disposed of the body out of panic. She admitted to tampering with evidence and dismembering the body but refused to admit murder.

During her testimony, the jury gasped in shock when she explained that she had to remove the icepick from Jimmy's eye in order to get his head in the pot to boil it.

———

Angela Stoldt showed no reaction when the jury came back after four hours of deliberation with their guilty verdict on all three charges. She was sentenced to a mandatory life term with no possibility of parole.

———

To this day, Angela Stoldt insists that she has been unjustly incarcerated for acting in self-defense. She indirectly maintains a blog explaining her grounds for mistrial, her explanation of self-defense, and claims that her sister, who testified against her, had been mentally, physically, and sexually abusive to her for her entire life.

CHAPTER 9
A TRAGIC DECEMBER

There was snow in the forecast for Bristol that Friday night. It was December 17, 2010, and twenty-five-year-old Joanna "Jo" Yeates was hoping for a white Christmas. She and her boyfriend, Greg Reardon, had just moved to Bristol in the east of England the previous year when the company they both worked for had relocated there. Once they settled in Bristol, Joanna took a job at Building Design Partnership as a Landscape Designer, the field in which she had received her postgraduate degree.

After work that Friday, Greg and Joanna met at the train station and kissed goodbye as Greg boarded the 5:00 train for Sheffield to visit his family before the holidays. Joanna, meanwhile, planned to spend a weekend alone in their quiet basement flat: Unit 1, 44 Canynge Road. It was to be her first night alone in the flat since they had moved in.

After seeing Greg off, Joanna walked back toward her home and stopped at the Bristol Ram Pub at around 6:00 for drinks with friends from work. The pub was busy and the mood was festive. It was an impromptu Christmas party. Joanna sipped her lager while listening to her colleagues complain about their bosses and they all talked about their plans for the holidays. Joanna's plans involved a trip to Hampshire to visit her family and making mince pies with her mother, as she had done every Christmas for as long as she could remember.

Joanna Yeates

By 8:00, Joanna bid her friends farewell and started the mile walk toward home. Along the way, she stopped at a Waitrose supermarket and looked around for something to cook for dinner but found nothing. She continued walking and popped into a corner shop, where she picked up two bottles of cider. Just before home, she stopped at a Tesco supermarket and bought a mozzarella, basil, and tomato pizza to cook when she arrived home.

———

Greg Reardon did his best to enjoy his time with his family in Sheffield but his mind was preoccupied. That Friday night when he arrived at his parents' house and called Joanna, she didn't pick up. Okay, he thought. Maybe she's just asleep already. But when she didn't answer any of his texts or calls all Saturday or Sunday morning, he was beginning to worry. Had he said something wrong? Was she avoiding him for some reason?

Sunday afternoon, Greg took the long train ride from Sheffield back down to Bristol and expected to see Joanna's smiling face at the train station to greet him, but she wasn't there. Anxious to find out what was wrong, Greg rushed to their flat and found the door unlocked. Although it was now after midnight, the lights were still on but there was no sign of Joanna.

Again, Greg called her cell phone – only to be hit with panic when it rang in the hallway. Her cell phone was tucked inside the pocket of her jacket, still hanging on a hook near the door. Then he noticed her glasses, her wallet, and her keys. They were all still in the flat, but where was Joanna?

Joanna's parents were startled to be woken up by a phone call after midnight. Confusion set in when the caller ID showed that their daughter's boyfriend was calling at such a late hour.

When Greg explained the situation to Joanna's parents, they told him to call the police straight away and they would drive up from Hampshire as quickly as they could.

———

By morning, Joanna's parents had reported her missing and Bristol Police began a thorough search of the area. Greg and Joanna's flat bordered Clifton Downs, a large park that had cliffs leading down to the River Avon. Beyond the river was Leigh Woods, a massive National Forest. There was an enormous amount of space to cover and, within days, the search became one of the largest in Bristol history.

Detectives searched the flat and found no sign of a struggle. No windows or doors had been broken. Nothing. The only thing out of the ordinary was a receipt from Tesco for a pizza – but there was no pizza and no packaging in the trash.

Joanna's friends and family did the best they could to assist in the search, putting up flyers all over the city and begging for any clues at all to help find her. The snow was falling harder as the days passed and her parents walked down the streets of the neighborhood, peering over fences and even tapping on the trunks of cars in case she had been tied up and held inside someone's trunk.

Right away, police questioned neighbors and friends she had seen that night. The friends Joanna had met at the Bristol Ram Pub said she was as happy as ever that night. Nothing seemed to be troubling her and they didn't notice anyone other than them-selves talking to her that night at all.

Neighbors from nearby flats, however, claimed to have heard a woman's screams at around 9:30 that Friday night. As nobody was quite sure where the screams were coming from, they didn't call the police.

Greg and Joanna's unit was a basement flat in a four-story building. The neighbors across the hall, Unit 2, were Tanja Morson and Vincent Tabak. The couple were questioned by detectives and Tanja explained that she was out-of-town all weekend, having traveled outside of Bristol for a Christmas work party. Vincent Tabak, however, told that he had gone out that evening to get some groceries, had a pizza and beer at home, and watched television. He said he didn't see or hear anything out of the ordinary the entire weekend.

The upstairs neighbor, sixty-five-year-old Christopher Jeffries, told detectives that he was home all Friday evening reading a book and heard nothing downstairs. Jeffries was a retired English teacher who didn't own a television and preferred to read from his extensive book collection. Jeffries had longish, wispy gray hair and seemed a bit eccentric. However, what detectives were most interested in was the fact that he was the landlord of the building. As landlord, Jeffries had keys for every unit.

———

Although the search for Joanna Yeates involved eighty detectives and civilian staff, police desperately needed the help of the public. They began Facebook campaigns and held press conferences to get the word out. Security camera footage was shown to the public of Joanna at the Bristol Ram Pub, Waitrose, and Tesco. Although hundreds of tips came in, nothing seemed to help.

It was Christmas Day and Joanna had been missing for eight days. Missing person flyers bearing her face and description were put up everywhere on the snowy streets of Bristol. Her friends and family were losing hope and were told by police to prepare for the worst. It was, without a doubt, the bleakest holiday ever for those close to her.

On Christmas afternoon, a couple walking their dog on Long-wood Lane in Fairland noticed a snow-covered mound just a few feet from the side of the road, next to a fence. Thinking nothing of it, they continued walking their dog. On the way back, they glanced again at the mound. This time, they noticed what seemed to be blue jeans protruding from the snow. A closer look revealed the body of a young woman curled up on her side, frozen in the snow.

Investigators arrived and found the body of Joanna Yeates. She was fully clothed except for one missing sock. Her postmortem examination revealed forty-three cuts and bruises on her body and that her nose had been broken, none of which had killed her. She had been manually strangled to death. There were no signs of sexual assault, but there were traces of DNA from someone other than Joanna. Interestingly, the postmortem examination showed that there were no signs of the pizza she had purchased in her stomach. Investigators determined that she had died that Friday night, had been killed elsewhere, and was dumped along the side of the road soon after her death.

————

Police announced that Joanna's body had been found and again turned to the media for help. They held a press conference and showed the sock she was wearing and asked the public for help to find the missing sock. They also showed the brand of pizza she bought on the night she went missing and asked for help to find the missing packaging.

With the help of investigators, the BBC television show Crimewatch filmed a recreation of the last known movements of Joanna before she was killed. The show offered a £10,000 reward for information leading to the arrest of her killer and The Sun Newspapers offered an additional £50,000. After the airing of the show, police received thousands of calls.

————

As the days passed since finding her body, detectives looked closer at Joanna's landlord, Christopher Jeffries. Since there was no sign of forced entry, investigators believed that Joanna had been murdered either by someone she knew and willingly let into her flat, or someone that had access to the flat. As landlord, Jeffries would have had a key to the flat and could have entered anytime he liked.

Detectives also learned that Jeffries had helped Greg work on his car earlier in the day that Friday, before he left for Sheffield. He knew that Joanna would have been alone all weekend. On December 30, Christopher Jeffries was arrested and brought in for questioning while a forensic team searched his flat.

Investigators packed up his entire book collection and several large boxes and bags of his belongings, then brought them in for analysis while television news crews filmed the event.

Within three hours of his arrest, Vincent Tabak, the neighbor that lived across the hall from Joanna and Greg, called detectives. He and his girlfriend had gone to Amsterdam for New Year's. Tabak told investigators that he saw the news of Jeffries' arrest and remembered something from that night that may be of help.

Tabak remembered that earlier that Friday evening, Jeffries' car had been parked in the driveway pointing one direction. The next morning, however, he noticed it had been backed in facing the opposite direction.

Detectives wanted to know more. On New Year's Eve, two detectives flew to Amsterdam to speak to Tabak in person and get a full statement. They met with Tabak in a hotel near the Amsterdam airport. During the interview, however, Tabak was uncertain of some details and vague on others. One thing, however, struck the detectives as particularly suspicious: he was overly interested in the forensic evidence and seemed to be concerned with how the investigation was proceeding. After speaking to Tabak for six hours, detectives asked him to provide a DNA sample to eliminate him as a suspect. Tabak protested. He was exceedingly reluctant to provide his DNA but, after some coaxing, he agreed and detectives retrieved his DNA.

———

Back in Bristol, Christopher Jeffries had been held in jail and interrogated for seventy-two hours before being released on bail. Although he was not officially charged with a crime, the tabloid newspapers throughout the United Kingdom followed him incessantly and labeled him an "odd eccentric character," a "peeping Tom," and painted him as a weirdo for being a fan of "dark and violent avant-garde films."

After the airing of the BBC Crimewatch reenactment, police received an anonymous call from a crying woman who was moved to tears by the show. It's unclear what information she gave to police but, just hours after the call, at 2:00 A.M. on January 20, Vincent Tabak was arrested.

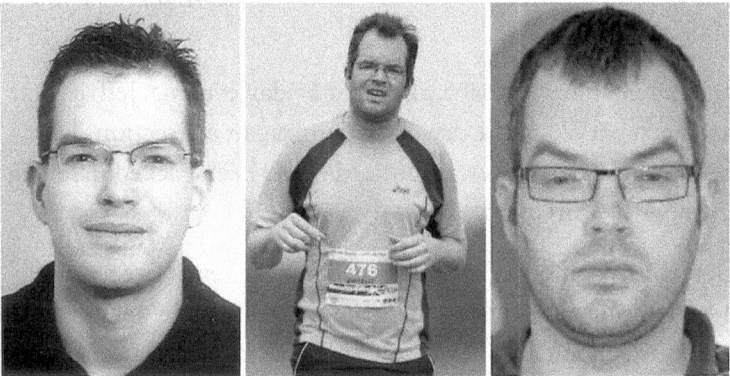

Vincent Tabak

Vincent Tabak was interrogated for ninety-six hours, during which he said very little. On January 22 he was formally charged with the murder of Joanna Yeates. His request for bail was denied.

Vincent Tabak was a thirty-two-year-old Dutch national that had been working in the United Kingdom as a people-flow engineer specializing in the movement of people in public spaces. His very specialized skill was in high demand. He had excelled in school and received a PhD. He was well-liked by his friends and colleagues, although many people described him as shy and introverted.

Forensic teams searched his home and found that he regularly watched sadistic and violent pornography on the internet, particularly that of women being choked during sex. He had watched it just before and immediately after Joanna had gone missing. Tabak also collected several images of a girl removing her pink top. The girl in the images bore a striking similarity to Joanna Yeates. When Joanna's body was found, she was wearing a top very similar to the girl in the photos.

Further searches of his computer and cell phone records showed that he often hired sex workers when he traveled for work throughout the United Kingdom and the United States.

Vincent Tabak had searched Google street view at the precise location on Longwood Lane where Joanna's body was found just days before her body was found there. Blood was found in the trunk of his car that matched Joanna's and the DNA that was found on Joanna's body matched his own.

Still, Tabak insisted that he had nothing to do with Joanna's murder and claimed that the police had fabricated the evidence against him, including the DNA. His hometown newspapers in the Netherlands believed him. His friends, family, and the Dutch media rallied behind him and raised money for his defense.

Detectives analyzed the movements of Vincent Tabak on the night that Joanna Yeates disappeared. That night, while his girlfriend was away, he drove across town to an Asda Supermarket. Security cameras showed him walking through the store, then exiting without buying anything. Moments later, he walked back into the store and bought some crisps, beer, and salt. After the purchase, he paused near the entrance of the store where he knew cameras were watching him and sent his girlfriend a text message: "I'm at Asda buying some crisps. It's boring without you."

To detectives, it was clearly an attempt to give himself an alibi. The store was well out of his way, requiring a drive. If he had wanted to buy beer, crisps, and salt, he could have simply walked to the corner shop near his home.

Three weeks after his arrest, Vincent Tabak confessed to a prison chaplain that he had killed Joanna, but he claimed it was an accident. He later pleaded guilty – but only to a charge of manslaughter. Prosecutors, however, weren't satisfied and wouldn't accept a manslaughter conviction. There was plenty of evidence against him and they insisted on trying him for murder. Forensic investigators also found that he had been using his computer to search about the difference between murder and manslaughter.

––––––––

During his trial, the court was not allowed to hear any evidence pertaining to his deviant porn surfing habits or his hiring of escorts. The judge didn't believe that it proved that the murder was premeditated, so it was not allowed. His defense took advantage of this and tried to portray Tabak as sexually naïve.

Tabak took the stand in his own defense and claimed that the death of Joanna Yeates was accidental. He said that he walked by her kitchen window as she was making dinner and she waved at him. When he waved back, she invited him in.

Tabak explained that he and Joanna chatted in the kitchen for ten to fifteen minutes and he interpreted her actions as flirtatious. When he went to kiss her, however, she screamed and his first reaction was to cover her mouth. When he removed his hand, he claimed she screamed again. Tabak explained that he panicked at her screams, put his hands around her throat, and accidentally strangled her to death.

During the thirteen days of the trial, Vincent Tabak failed to answer eighty of the questions posed to him by the prosecution. On October 28, 2011, after fourteen hours of deliberation, the jury found him guilty of murder. Vincent Tabak was given a life sentence with a minimum term of twenty years in prison.

———

Despite the guilty verdict of Vincent Tabak and the charges dropped against Christopher Jeffries, Jeffries continued to be vilified by the tabloid press. As a result, he hired a law firm and sued eight newspapers for libel. Jeffries received substantial payment for damages from The Sun, The Daily Mirror, The Sunday Mirror, The Daily Record, The Daily Mail, The Daily Express, The Daily Star, and The Scotsman. In addition, for reporting information that could have prejudiced the trial, The Daily Mirror and The Sun were found guilty of contempt of court.

CHAPTER 10
THE COUNT

The night clubs of Sunset Boulevard in West Hollywood are notorious for launching the careers of countless rock legends. Clubs like Whisky a Go Go, The Roxy Theatre, Rainbow Bar and Grill, and Troubadour have hosted music groups for decades. Some have been in operation since the late 1950s. Even today, the Sunset Strip is crowded with young Los Angelinos having a good time or hoping to catch a glimpse of a celebrity every weekend night.

On Saturday, January 12, 1985, Lisa Mather put on her black skirt over her purple spandex tights and buckled her silver-studded black pumps in preparation for a night out with her friends on the Sunset Strip. Lisa left her mother a note saying that she was going to hang out by Whisky a Go Go and would be out late, but not to worry. Although they weren't yet old enough to get into the clubs, Lisa, Aimee, and Anthony were going to have the night of their lives walking up and down the Strip.

Lisa and her friends spent the night club-hopping and meeting with friends outside of the Rainbow and the Whisky. Along with the other underage kids that couldn't get into the clubs, they just listened to the music bellowing out of the clubs and danced and drank in the abandoned construction site next door. But when police showed up to break up the underage party, the kids scattered. As they ran from the construction site, Aimee and Anthony lost sight of Lisa.

For the next several hours, Aimee and Anthony walked up and down the Sunset Strip checking all the usual clubs, but they couldn't find Lisa. The last time they remembered seeing her, she was talking to a tall, skinny, older boy wearing all black, with hair-sprayed and back-combed "rocker hair." The description fit pretty much every male on the Strip.

As the hazy red dawn broke over Los Angeles, Aimee and Anthony had given up hope of finding their friend. It was time to call Lisa's mother and let her know they couldn't find her.

Lisa's mother waited patiently for her daughter to come home. Although it was unlike her to stay out like that, she was eighteen and could do what she wanted. But early the following week, when she still hadn't come home or called, Betty Mather called the police to report her daughter missing.

Lisa Ann Mather had recently graduated from Van Nuys High School and was attending beauty school when she vanished. Although police initially suspected that she had simply run off with a boy for a few days, Betty Mather knew it was more than that. Something was wrong. Despite the lack of effort by the police, Lisa's friends and family put up flyers all over West Hollywood, specifically near the clubs along Sunset Boulevard.

Lisa Ann Mather

Eventually, police began to take the case more seriously and started their investigation. Lisa's sister, Rosalyn, told police about an incident that had happened a few weeks before Lisa went missing.

While she, Lisa, and Aimee were cruising up and down Sunset Strip, a young man invited them to a house party in the Holly-wood Hills. Although they didn't know the man, they accepted the invitation in hopes of meeting celebrities.

As the man drove them erratically along Mulholland Drive toward the party, Rosalyn asked him to slow down. He snapped back at her, "Listen, bitch. You better shut the fuck up or I'm gonna make you walk the streets like a whore!"

When they arrived at a house in the hills, the man told the girls to wait in the car while he went into the house.

When he emerged, he told the two younger girls that they could stay, but he took Rosalyn back down the hill to the Sunset Strip and dropped her on a street corner. Scared that he and whoever was in the house had kidnapped Aimee and Lisa, Rosalyn called the police.

At the time, the police determined that the two girls were safe and nothing illegal was going on. But weeks later, now that Lisa was missing, Rosalyn believed the people at that house may have had something to do with her disappearance.

Rosalyn talked detectives into returning to the house to question the residents, but again, they found nothing wrong and there was no sign of Lisa.

A week later, police received an anonymous tip from someone who claimed that a young girl matching Lisa's description was being held against her will in a Las Vegas hotel room and was being forced into prostitution. The caller knew in which hotel and room number to find the girl. Los Angeles police collaborated with Las Vegas police to investigate the lead. Although they did find a young girl, it wasn't Lisa – it had been a fifteen-year-old runaway from Wyoming.

One month after Lisa's disappearance, Betty Mather received a phone call from a man asking to speak with Lisa. The call startled her. Was this a man that didn't know that Lisa was missing? Or was it some lunatic taunting her?

The caller then explained that his van had been stolen while parked near the Sunset Strip a month ago, around the same time that Lisa had gone missing. Several weeks later, he retrieved the stolen van and found a matchbook inside. Inside the flap of the matchbook was Lisa's name and phone number. The man was trying to find out who had stolen his van.

Police briefly considered the man a suspect. Investigators examined the van and found no traces of blood and no indication that Lisa had been in it other than the matchbook. The man had indeed reported his van stolen and had a solid alibi for the night Lisa disappeared. Although they no longer suspected the owner of the van, police hypothesized that whoever had stolen the van may have used it to abduct Lisa.

Lisa's mother verified that the handwriting inside matched Lisa's. The logo on the cover of the matchbook displayed the name of a restaurant in Marina Del Rey, more than ten miles away from the Sunset Strip, but employees of the restaurant didn't recognize photos of Lisa.

———

Lisa had been missing for seven months when the notorious Night Stalker, Richard Ramirez, was captured. Ramirez faced thirteen counts of murder and, for a brief time, was thought to be a suspect in the disappearance of Lisa Mather. Ramirez, however, had a completely different modus operandi: he terrorized and murdered people in their own homes. He didn't abduct young girls off the street.

———

Almost two years after she went missing, on December 3, 1986, Paul Yettaw was hiking through the woods of Coldwater Canyon, just north of Mulholland Drive and a few miles above Sunset Boulevard, when he discovered a human skull, a spine, and leg bones covered lightly with branches and dirt. A rope twisted through the skeleton and was tied to the base of a tree on a steep incline. A pair of rusted handcuffs hung from a tree branch above.

When investigators arrived, they recovered additional bones that had slipped down the hill or had been moved by animals. The scapula, or shoulder blade, had evidence of a puncture wound. Although they could not determine the cause of death, they knew it was the body of a female between the ages of sixteen and twenty-three.

Loops in the rope attached to the tree indicated that her legs and arms and been bound and she was spread-eagle on the ground. Tent spikes were found nearby, indicating that there had been a campsite. Various articles of women's clothing were found several yards uphill from the skeleton, indicating that the girl had been naked while she was bound to the tree.

Using dental records, investigators confirmed that it was the body of Lisa Ann Mather.

———

Despite the lack of physical evidence at the scene, police believed they knew who killed Lisa Mather – and he was already in prison. Just sixteen days after Lisa had gone missing, Edmund Arne Matthews had been arrested for two rapes. Both of the rapes had occurred the year prior at the same campsite where Lisa's body was found. When Lisa's friend, Anthony, was shown a photo lineup, he identified Matthews as the man that Lisa had been talking to on the night she went missing.

———

Edmund Arne Matthews was twenty-eight years old and living in a tent when Lisa disappeared. He frequented the Sunset Strip and was known for wandering from bar to bar wearing a long black cape, fancying himself a vampire, and calling himself "The Count." He often told young, gullible girls that he had been a drummer for Ted Nugent and claimed to share an apartment with Nancy Sinatra. Matthews spoke regularly about his obsession with Satanism, archangels, and his "Dr. Jekyll and Mr. Hyde" personality.

Edmund Arne Matthews

On October 13, 1984, just three months before the murder, Matthews lured a twenty-year-old girl named Daniella away from the Sunset Strip to a party in the Hollywood Hills. There was no party. Matthews pulled her to his campsite on the hillside, handcuffed her, tore off her clothes, put chains around her ankles, and raped her for hours before releasing her.

Two months later, Matthews coaxed another young girl named Janet from the Rainbow Bar and Grill. When he got her near his campsite, he knocked her to the ground and choked her. The terrified young girl urinated herself out of fear. Matthews bound her with her scarf and his own shoestrings. He ripped her clothes off and told her of his fantasy of tying up a girl and keeping her at his campsite as his sex slave. He then held a machete up to her face and told her he planned to kill her. Instead, he raped her four times that night before releasing her.

———

Edmund Matthews was arrested for the rapes sixteen days after Lisa Mather went missing as he carried a shovel and lantern from his campsite. Lisa's case, however, was only a missing person at the time and the police had no way of linking him to her murder.

———

When detectives visited Matthews in prison to question him about the murder of Lisa Mather, he said he didn't recognize the name. When he was shown her photo, however, he turned his head in shame. He told the detective that he'd had far too much to drink the night he met Lisa and he could barely remember anything. He claimed that he kept having "spinning blackouts," but he remembered coming down the hill that night thinking that he may have killed someone with a rope.

Matthews said he stayed at a friend's house that night. The next morning, he walked back up the hill to his campsite and saw the girl dead, tied by her neck to the tree. He claimed that he couldn't even remember how he had tied her up. He covered her body with bits of shrubbery and walked back down the hill.

Matthews told investigators that three days later, he borrowed a shovel and went back to the scene intending to bury her. However, he couldn't untie the rope. Instead, he just covered the body with more pieces of bushes, leaves, and dirt. As he walked down the hill, he was arrested for the two prior rapes. The arresting officers had no idea that Lisa's corpse was tied to a tree just a few hundred feet away.

———

One month later, Edmund Matthews wrote a statement for detectives detailing the events of the night as he remembered them. He wanted to plead guilty and avoid the death penalty. Matthews explained that he met Lisa at Whiskey a Go Go and they went across the street for drinks. Later they took a taxi to Harvard Middle School, just up the hill, where he knew a way to hop the fence and go swimming in their pool. He claimed they had consensual sex against the ladder of the diving board. That was when he invited her to his campsite, which was within walking distance of the school.

Once at the campsite, Matthews claimed they had consensual sex again. This time, she agreed to let him tie her up to a tree. He wound the rope around the tree and around her neck, then went back to his tent to find a lantern. While looking for the lantern, he said he heard her squeal. When he ran back to the tree, she was on her back. She had slipped and was choking. He said it had rained recently and the ground around his campsite was slippery. He claimed she had slipped while the rope was around her neck and she was choking to death.

Matthews wrote that he panicked. He rushed to her and tried to untie her but couldn't. As he was trying to untie her, she had stopped breathing. He checked for a pulse and there was none. When he realized she was dead, he panicked. He said he ran back down the hill and stayed the night at a friend's house.

Matthews' story, however, didn't match the way the body had been positioned. The rope was bound tightly to the base of the tree. She wasn't standing. There was no way for her to have fallen and choked herself accidentally. His story also didn't match the testimony his two previous rape victims told. They were brought to his campsite unwillingly and would never have followed him into the woods. Lisa's family knew that she, also, would never have followed him willingly, either.

Matthews wrote in the letter that he was suicidal, depressed, and tired. The trial of Edmund Arne Matthews was delayed for almost two years as his defense team argued that the sex was consensual and not rape. A first-degree murder case with rape required prosecutors to seek the death penalty. If the rape charge was removed, he would only be sentenced to life in prison if convicted. The requests to have the rape charge removed, however, were denied.

———

The trial began in January 1991. For thirty-eight days, Matthews claimed that the death of Lisa Mather was just a series of unfortunate accidents. His two prior rape victims, however, testified about the horrors of their ordeals with Matthews.

On February 14, 1991, Edmund Matthews was found guilty of first-degree murder, including special circumstances. Although he was eligible for the death penalty, he was sentenced to life in prison without parole.

Edmund Matthew's mother approached Lisa's mother, offered her condolences, and hugged her. She asked, "Can you please find it in your heart to forgive him?"

Betty Mather returned the embrace and replied, "My heart goes out to you, but I can't forgive him. You can see your son every day. I will never see my daughter again."

After the trial, Betty Mather expressed her disappointment with the sentence of life in prison, telling the Los Angeles Times, "I think he should have been killed for the way he killed my child. I will never have my daughter again. His mother can still visit him, but I don't have my daughter. I think our system is the worst."

CHAPTER 11
ANGELIC

Karlie Pearce-Stevenson had spent her entire life in Alice Springs in the Northern Territory of Australia. The small town is extremely remote and sits in the dead center of the continent, in what is referred to as the Red Centre, the country's interior desert. Alice Springs is the midpoint between the larger cities of Darwin to the north and Adelaide to the south, both of which are more than a fifteen-hour drive through vast expanses of barren red desert.

Karlie enjoyed life in Alice Springs, but the twenty-year-old longed for a larger city with more opportunities where she could raise her two-year-old daughter, Khandalyce.

Karlie's mother, family, and friends were sad to see her go, but they knew it was what she wanted to do. They were skeptical, however, of who she chose to leave town with. Karlie's new boyfriend, Daniel Holdom, was fifteen years older than Karlie and her family really didn't know much about the man. But Karlie was determined. In mid-2008, without any long good-byes, Karlie, Khandalyce, and Holdom left the small town to find a new life.

Initially, Karlie called and texted her friends and family on a regular basis, often expressing her regret about leaving the small town. But by the summer of 2009, Karlie's communications had mysteriously stopped. All calls or text messages suddenly went unanswered and, after several months of not hearing from her daughter, Karlie's mother, Colleen Povey, called the police. On September 4, she filed a missing person report with the Northern Territory Police.

Karlie & Khandalyce Pearce-Stevenson / Daniel Holdom

Karlie was an adult and could do what she pleased, but police took the investigation seriously and did their best to locate Karlie and Khandalyce. Investigators checked Karlie's banking records and could see that the account was still active and used regularly. Nothing seemed out of the ordinary. They also saw that her welfare payments issued by Centrelink were still being cashed.

There was also a record that she had been pulled over by police for speeding on the Stuart Highway north of Adelaide in November 2008, but almost a year had passed since then.

Still, looking for further proof of life, detectives contacted the person that was last seen with Karlie and Khandalyce: Daniel Holdom. Investigators located and called Holdom, who assured them that Karlie was very much alive and well. He passed the phone to Karlie, who spoke to investigators and reassured them, "I'm fine. I just don't want to speak to my family anymore."

With that, investigators were satisfied that Karlie was indeed alive but just in need of her privacy. They relayed the news to her mother. Colleen was sad and confused that her daughter didn't want to speak to her family or friends any longer, but at the same time, she was relieved that Karlie and Khandalyce were alive. What none of them knew, however, was that the woman that had spoken to investigators was not Karlie.

———

In August 2010, two young men riding dirt bikes through the bushland of the Belangelo State Forest, almost 1,800 miles from Alice Springs near Sydney, came across a gruesome discovery – human bones making up an entire female skeleton. Nearby, investigators found pieces of jewelry, a sock, and a printed t-shirt with the word "Angelic" written on it.

Initially there was speculation that the body may have been a victim of Ivan Milat, the serial killer who had murdered young women throughout Australia from 1989 to 1993. However, forensic examination of the skeleton determined that this murder was much more recent and had most likely taken place within the past two years.

Using the structure of the skull, forensic anthropologists were able to put together a composite drawing of what the victim may have looked like. They released it to the public along with photos of the t-shirt. The evidence, however, didn't seem to match any active missing person reports. No one came forward to say the girl looked familiar. With no clues, the case went cold. For the next five years, the police and media referred to the mysterious girl as "Angel."

Composite drawing of the victim / Angelic t-shirt design

———

Several years had passed since anyone had had contact with Karlie Pearce-Stevenson when her mother suddenly got a text message. The message came from Karlie's cell phone and Colleen had no reason to believe it wasn't her. Karlie wanted her mother to know that she was okay, but she and Khandalyce needed money. Colleen was eager to help her daughter and quickly wired her $500. The same request came several more times over the next year and each time she wired more money.

Colleen Povey was suffering from breast cancer and pleaded with her daughter to come back home to visit. Each time Karlie promised she would come home. Unfortunately, Colleen died in 2012 without ever knowing the true fate of her daughter and granddaughter.

On July 14, 2015, five years after the skeleton was found in the Belangelo State Forest, a man traveling on a remote highway east of Adelaide discovered an abandoned suitcase along the side of the road. When he pulled over to get a closer look, he found a small quilt and young child's clothes inside. Nearby, further off the side of the road and behind a tree, he found more children's clothing: a pink dress, a fur-trimmed coat, a tiny black tutu, and a tiny Dora the Explorer shirt. When the man looked closer at the clothes inside the suitcase, he got the shock of his life. Poking through the fabric was a jawbone. As he dug deeper through the clothes, he found a tiny human skeleton laying in the fetal position.

From the size of the bones, investigators determined that the victim was female and approximately two to four years old. It was impossible to believe that a toddler of that age had disappeared without anyone noticing, but the tiny girl matched no missing person reports.

Five years had passed since the body in the Belangelo State Forest was found. The toddler in the suitcase was found 680 miles away from the first body in a different state. It was no wonder that law enforcement hadn't linked the two cases.

Authorities wouldn't release the official cause of death of the toddler, instead opting to only tell the media that the young girl found in the suitcase had died a "violent death under terrible circumstances."

Again, investigators reached out to the public to help identify the girl. The only clues that they had available were the Lanza brand suitcase and the clothes found inside the suitcase. The brands of the clothing were mostly mass produced and sold in

Kmart stores throughout Australia. However, one item in the suitcase – the small quilt – appeared to be handmade.

South Australia Police held a televised press conference where they dressed a tiny mannequin in clothing identical to that found in the suitcase and displayed the same brand of suitcase in which the body was found. They also released photos of each piece of clothing and the handmade quilt, then set up a hotline for tips. The death of the toddler was heart wrenching and the news reached all across Australia.

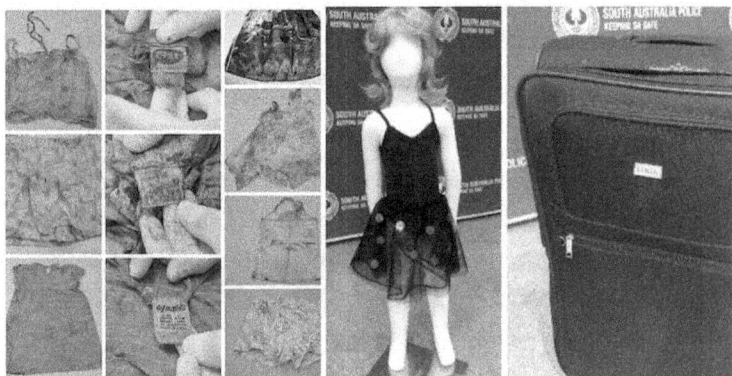

Clothes found at scene / mannequin and suitcase shown at press conference

Immediately the tips poured in from the nearby tiny town of Wynarka. Although the town had only seventy-five residents, fifteen of them called to say they had seen a Caucasian man in his sixties wheeling a similar suitcase through town three months earlier, in late April.

More than 1,000 calls poured in to the Crime Stoppers hotline throughout August and September, but it wasn't until October that police got their first useful tip. A woman from Adelaide, more than eighty miles from where the body was found, recognized the pink dress that had been found in the suitcase. Incredibly, the woman had met Karlie and Khandalyce in a shopping mall in Adelaide and taken a photo of Khandalyce wearing an identical pink dress. The meeting, however, had taken place seven years earlier, in November 2008.

Tanya Weber had been a friend of Karlie's back in Alice Springs and had heard the news of the toddler's body being found. Fearing the worst, she rummaged through boxes of old photos until she found a photo of Khandalyce in her stroller. In the photo, behind Khandalyce's head, was the same handmade quilt she had seen on the news.

When Khandalyce was born, she had been given a neonatal heel prick in order to take a blood sample. DNA from the skeletal remains were compared to the blood taken during the heel prick and it was a match. The body in the suitcase was positively identified as Khandalyce.

A national DNA search using Khandalyce's DNA matched her mother's remains. Karlie Pearce-Stevenson was positively identified as the body found in Belangelo State Forest.

———

Detectives now knew that Karlie and Khandalyce had been murdered and had most likely already been dead when they were first reported missing six years earlier. Two questions remained, however: who killed them and who had detectives spoken to on the phone, years earlier, that had claimed to be Karlie?

Detectives began their investigation by attempting to retrace Karlie's steps since she first left Alice Springs. They knew that she had driven from one end of the continent to the other and had to have stayed in motels or campgrounds along the way. Investigators reached out to any campgrounds, landlords, or motel operators who might have remembered the young girl traveling with her daughter and an older man, but none reached out.

They also needed to speak with the man with whom Karlie had left Alice Springs, Daniel Holdom. Forty-one-year-old Holdom was the obvious suspect and wasn't hard to find. It was an ominous premonition of things to come when detectives discovered he was already in jail for sexually assaulting a young girl in a campground. Having Holdom in custody, however, gave investigators time to look closely into his background.

Daniel Holdom had a long history of drug addiction and abuse of women and children. His record showed that he had sexually assaulted an eight-year-old girl and had attempted to strangle a woman. He was also accused of stalking another.

Search warrants were issued for several homes across Australia, where Holdom had lived throughout the years. It didn't take long for investigators to know they had the killer.

In one of his homes where he lived in Canberra, they found a diary written in Holdom's handwriting where he fantasized about sexually abusing children. In the diary, he used specific children's names and ages as he detailed his sadistic desires. Words such as "rape" and "forced" were peppered throughout. His fingerprints were all over the diary.

Police also learned that, just months before Daniel Holdom met Karlie, he was involved in a fatal car accident. Holdom was driving through the interior desert of central Australia with his then-girlfriend, Hazel Passmore, and her two young children. When he swerved to avoid a kangaroo in the road, the SUV rolled several times.

The crash left her two children, seven-year-old Ryan and nine-year-old Willow, dead. Hazel Passmore lost her leg above the knee and was confined to a wheelchair for the rest of her life. Holdom escaped unharmed. After the incident, Passmore sued Holdom for negligence, seeking unspecified damages for her losses. While Hazel Passmore spent months in the hospital and rehab, Holdom began his relationship with Karlie.

Detectives soon learned, however, that just after Karlie and Khandalyce went missing, Holdom and Passmore had reconciled.

Investigators served a search warrant on the home of Hazel Passmore and questioned her. During her initial interview, she gave very little detail of her relationship with Daniel Holdom and denied any involvement in the murders. Passmore, however, had uploaded photos from a classic car show onto her Facebook timeline. In the forefront of the photos, Khandalyce Pearce-Stevenson could be seen walking around the cars. The photos, however, were taken in Alice Springs, just before Karlie and Khandalyce had left town.

Photos of Khandalyce from Hazel Passmore's Facebook page / Hazel Passmore

When questioned a second time by investigators, Passmore hired a lawyer. She and her lawyer agreed to a deal with prosecutors. She would tell them what she knew in an "induced statement," meaning she couldn't be prosecuted for any involvement in the case.

Knowing she was immune from prosecution, Hazel Passmore told police that Daniel Holdom had admitted to her that he had killed Karlie and Khandalyce. She initially didn't believe him and thought he was just joking, so she didn't report the murders to the police. Passmore also admitted that she was the woman that spoke to investigators and claimed to be Karlie. She had been the one that had been accessing Karlie's bank accounts and had even gone into the Centrelink offices in her wheelchair, posing as Karlie. Through the years, the couple had withdrawn almost $100,000 from Karlie's accounts.

Passmore explained that she had no idea that Karlie and Khandalyce were dead – she thought that she and Holdom were simply having an affair behind Karlie's back. It wasn't until she discovered Karlie's Medicaid card and Khandalyce's birth certificate that she had realized what he had done and confronted him about it.

"I was yelling and screaming 'What the fuck is this shit?!' I was going off my nut and he pulled me inside, literally by the scruff of the neck.

He threw the chair, and he starts shaking me and he's like, 'She's disappeared, she's gone, she's gone.' And I'm like, 'What do you mean she's gone?' And he's like, 'She's dead, she's dead.'"

Passmore also provided telling insight into Holdom's sexual preferences. She said that he had shown an interest in child abuse and bestiality websites and often asked her to recount her own child abuse to him. He also liked to write his own rape stories.

Hazel Passmore had given an SD card to her sister years earlier and told her, "If anything happens to me, you need to give this to police." When police searched the SD card, they found photos from the Belangelo State Forest that Hazel had copied from Daniel Holdom's computer.

The horrific photos showed Karlie Pearce-Stevenson at the time of her death, clearly showing the "Angelic" t-shirt she had been wearing. Some of the photos also showed Daniel Holdom's arm in the periphery, putting him at the scene of the crime. The photos had shown that Holdom had sexually abused Karlie using a bottle before her death. He finally killed her by stepping on her throat, crushing her trachea. Holdom had taken photos as he raped and murdered Karlie and kept them on his computer as trophies.

Before he murdered Karlie, Holdom had dropped Khandalyce off with his relatives. Afterward, he picked her up and told his relatives he was driving the girl to her grandmother's home. Instead, he drove four hours west to the small town of Narrandera, where he purchased duct tape and dish cloths at a supermarket during the journey.

Police recovered a motel receipt where he had signed in as one adult and one child. Detectives believe he had stuffed dish cloths into her mouth and duct taped her mouth shut before raping and suffocating Khandalyce in the Narrandera motel. He then stuffed her tiny body into the suitcase and drove another eight hours west toward Hazel Passmore's home.

Before he reached his destination, Holdom tossed the suitcase on the side of the road near the remote town of Wynarka, where it sat untouched for more than five years.

Daniel Holdom

Daniel Holdom's cell phone records had shown his location all along the way, placing him in Belangelo State Forest at the time of Karlie's death and following to the exact location where he dumped the suitcase in Wynarka. He was officially charged with the murders of Karlie and Khandalyce Pearce-Stevenson on December 15, 2015.

Holdom initially pleaded guilty to the two murders, then at the last minute tried to retract his guilty plea of Khandalyce's murder. The judge, however, denied his retraction and on November 30, 2018, Daniel Holdom was sentenced to two consecutive life sentences without the chance of parole.

Hazel Passmore eventually received a $1,000,000 settlement in her suit against Holdom for the car crash that killed her children and severed her left leg.

CHAPTER 12
THE BEARS

Born in 1941, Susan Barnes grew up in Phoenix, Arizona, as the city began its rapid sprawl into the suburbs. Her father, a wealthy newspaper executive, provided Susan with the most comfortable life money could buy at the time, but he knew something was wrong. He and his wife knew their daughter was mentally ill. Her speech and thinking were disorganized and she often had delusional beliefs where she saw or heard things that weren't really there. Susan, however, disagreed and believed she had special powers. She called them her psychic abilities or mystical powers. She could see the future and the past. Unfortunately, a clinical psychiatrist disagreed with her parents and told them not to worry: that Susan was just an eccentric young woman.

In the late 1950s, Susan married a wealthy businessman and they lived a luxurious life in Scottsdale, Arizona, with their two sons. As the boys grew into their teen years, however, Susan became disillusioned with the marriage and her eyes wandered. She began having casual sex with young men, many of which were classmates of her own children. By the end of the 1960s, her husband finally gave up and demanded a divorce.

Throughout the 1970s, she continued her sexual exploits and became involved in the free-love, hippie culture of the time, having more than 150 sexual partners. Susan had given up a posh life of golfing and country clubs for a life of dark and seedy drug dens.

The first time she used LSD, Susan woke the next morning to find the walls of her own home had been painted with strange triangles and her name scribbled throughout the home. She had cut off almost all contact with her family. It was a regular occurrence for her to be high on LSD, hashish, peyote, mescaline, or whatever she could get her hands on. The more drugs she did, the more her mental illness took hold of her life.

At a Thanksgiving day party in 1977, Susan met an amateur marijuana dealer named James Clifford Carson. Although Carson was nine years younger than her, married, and had a four-year-old daughter, he too had recently begun to drift away from his domestic life and into the hippie counterculture. When he met Susan, he was mesmerized. He was fascinated by her free-spirited, bohemian lifestyle and she felt the same about him. They both had an instant animal magnetism toward each other and, from that point forward, nothing else mattered.

———

At a young age, James had been diagnosed with a rare bone disease that left him needing crutches during his early school years. His disability made him the target of bullies, but by high school he had overcome the illness and went on to study Chinese Philosophy in Iowa, where he met his wife, Lynn. While Lynn went on to get her master's degree, James stayed home to raise their baby daughter, Jennifer. James was a good father and treasured every moment he spent with Jennifer – but that had all changed when he met Susan Barnes.

James's attraction to Susan was overwhelming. Within months of meeting her, he had divorced his wife, Lynn, and married Susan. Despite her strange demeanor, Susan was everything he had ever dreamed of.

Drugs and mental illness consumed Susan Carson. Her delusions and paranoia were all she thought about. After a particularly intense LSD trip, Susan became convinced that she was a witch and was possessed by the devil. She believed that there was a hole in the top of her head where bad vibes could be poured into her skull. She was convinced that the hole had been created by electrical appliances.

James did his best to calm his wife and reassure her that she wasn't a witch at all. Instead, he insisted, she was a yogi and the hole in her head was a sign that she had been chosen by God to receive messages directly from him.

Weekends for four-year-old Jennifer Carson meant that she would spend Saturday and Sunday with her father and her new step-mother, Susan Barnes Carson. James and Susan's home was void of any furniture except for a waterbed in the bedroom. The rest of the tiny home was filled with potted plants. Jennifer slept on the floor, in a sleeping bag. Susan, however, wanted nothing to do with the little girl. Susan often called her a demon and told her that demons needed to be killed. Susan was a vegetarian and when Jennifer asked for a baloney sandwich, she was told that she was doomed to fry in hell because she ate meat.

One Sunday evening, when Jennifer returned home to her mother, Lynn noticed red welts on her daughter's back. Several long scrape marks traced down the center of her back, some of which had broken the skin. When she asked Jennifer how she got the welts, she told her mother that she had asked her father's new wife, Susan, to give her a back rub before she went to bed. Just like her mother did. Instead, Susan dug her fingernails into the girl's back. At that point, Lynn knew she had to get her daughter out of that situation.

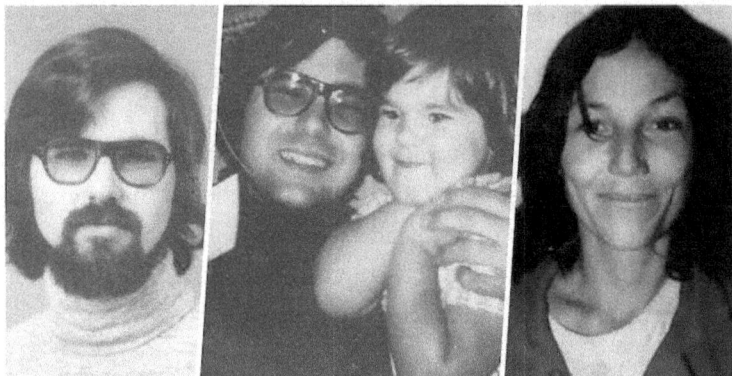

James Carson / with daughter Jennifer / Susan Barnes Carson

Lynn had heard that James and Susan were planning a year-long trip to Europe and worried that they would try to take Jennifer with them. She knew that if they took Jennifer out of the country, it would be the last time she would ever see her daughter. Before they had a chance, Lynn sent Jennifer to live with relatives in California.

———

In 1979, James and Susan left on a year-long trip where they traveled to the United Kingdom, France, Israel, and India. When they returned to the United States in 1980, they had both gone through a dramatic transformation. They were no longer James and Susan Carson. Instead, they had become Michael Bear and Suzan Bear. They both converted to Islam while in Jerusalem, but with their own psychotic interpretation of the Koran.

Two days after their return to the United States, they had moved to San Francisco and Suzan was arrested for public nudity and possession of marijuana. She pleaded guilty to the charge and received six months of probation. They lived in the infamous Haight Ashbury area of San Francisco, made famous for being the epicenter of the hippie counterculture in the late 1960s and early 1970s.

The arrest had given the couple a strong hatred for government, law enforcement, and any kind of authority figure and they had vowed never to pay taxes again.

Suzan and Michael immersed themselves in the hippie culture and reached out to easily influenced young people in the area, many of which were runaways, and attempted to create their own cult.

Their beliefs were based on vegetarianism, pacifism, and yoga, but leaned heavily on their misguided version of Islam. They preached mysticism, anarchy, and excessive use of psychedelic drugs. But, most importantly, they believed they had been tasked by God to rid the world of witches, homosexuals, and those who supported abortion.

One of their first followers was a twenty-three-year-old girl named Keryn Barnes. Keryn was an aspiring actress that had recently moved to San Francisco from Georgia. She was young, attractive, and easily persuaded by Michael and Suzan. As Michael and Keryn became closer, however, Suzan's jealousy triggered her psychosis. When Michael told Suzan that he wanted the young girl to become his second wife, it tipped her sanity over the edge.

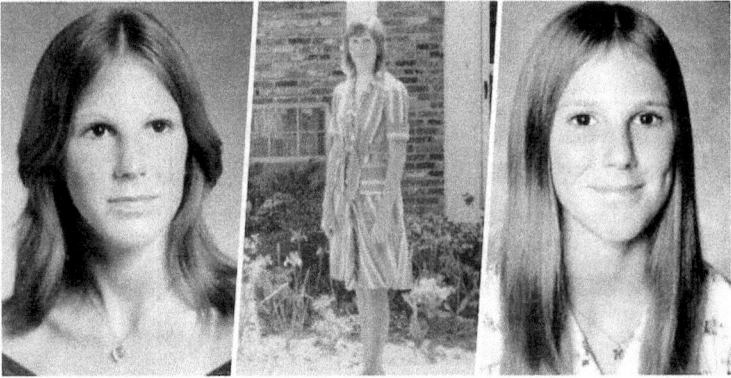

Keryn Barnes

Forty-year-old Suzan told her husband that she was having psychic visions about Keryn. She could see through Keryn's sweet demeanor and could envision her true image. Keryn, she proclaimed, was a psychic vampire. She was a witch that had cast a spell on her to steal her strength, beauty, and cosmic power. Suzan made it clear to her husband that the young, beautiful girl needed to die.

On the night of January 14, 1981, as Keryn Barnes slept on the floor of her apartment at 825 Shrader Street, Suzan Bear took a cast iron frying pan from the stove, shoved it at her husband, and snarled, "She's a witch! Do it!" Michael beat Keryn over the head with the frying pan until she was almost unrecognizable. He then took a paring knife and sliced her twice across the throat. Suzan wasn't satisfied. Keryn was still making gurgling sounds. She was still alive. Suzan picked up the knife and stabbed her in the torso eleven more times.

———

Police were called to the scene the next day when a plumber that was due for a repair discovered Keryn's body on the floor.

Throughout the home, investigators found nonsensical ranting messages written on the walls, many with the name "Suzan" scribbled beneath.

Although there were no witnesses to the murder, neighbors were well aware of the strange couple that had been staying with Keryn Barnes and told police what they knew. The neighbors knew them as Suzan and Michael Bear, who referred to themselves as "vegetarian Moslem warriors" and didn't believe in electricity or government of any kind. They said the couple had been traveling throughout California selling marijuana and preaching that they were on a mission from God to rid the world of witches. They also said that Michael had been trying to get a book of their twisted beliefs published. A close friend of Keryn Barnes told police that he believed that both Suzan and Michael were schizophrenic.

Investigators researched the names Michael and Suzan Bear but found nothing. No driver's license. No social security card. Nothing. Michael and Suzan fled the home and made their way north to Grant's Pass, in southern Oregon, where they laid low in a remote cabin for several months. Suzan wanted to be as far away as possible from any large city because she had been having visions that a nuclear war would happen any day.

When Michael finally convinced Suzan that it was safe to come out of hiding, the couple left the cabin and traveled to New Mexico, back to Oregon, and then settled in Humboldt County, California, in March 1982, halfway between San Francisco and the southern border of Oregon.

Both Suzan and Michael got jobs on a marijuana farm in the tiny town of Alderpoint, where they were tasked with cultivating the plants and keeping the farm secure. Michael was given a .22 caliber rifle and patrolled the farm to keep away anyone that wanted to steal the crops.

In May 1982, while keeping watch on the farm, Michael got into an argument with twenty-seven-year-old Clarke Stephens, who also worked on the farm. Suzan became unhinged during the altercation and screamed to Michael that Stephens was a demon and had sexually abused her. He needed to die. Michael did as his infuriated wife commanded and shot Stephens twice in the head and once in the chest, killing him instantly.

Michael and Suzan dragged Clarke's body through the marijuana fields and deep into the woods, where they covered him in chicken manure and lit him on fire. Although there were no police around as they burned the body, their drug-fueled paranoia got the best of them. They believed that the police were looking for them, left all their belongings, and ran through the woods.

When Clarke's friends and co-workers reported him missing, police found his charred remains in the woods along with the backpacks that Michael and Suzan had left behind. Inside the backpacks they found a notebook. It was a hand-written manifesto. It detailed the Bears' psychotic beliefs and their intention to rid the world of witches, including then-President Ronald Reagan, California Governor Jerry Brown, and television personality Johnny Carson.

———

Again, investigators were given the names Michael and Suzan Bear but couldn't find a record of them in any government databases. Co-workers, however, were able to provide an accurate physical description. Authorities throughout California were shown a composite drawing of Michael's face and were told to be on the lookout for the psychotic couple.

Suzan & Michael Bear / Police sketch of Michael Bear

Six months had passed without a clue as to the whereabouts of Michael or Suzan Bear. In November 1982, Michael was hitch-hiking in Los Angeles when an acquaintance that knew he was wanted for murder noticed Michael on the side of the road. Rather than give him a ride, the man called Los Angeles police.

That morning, a Los Angeles police bulletin had been released for officers to be on the lookout for an unrelated sexual assault suspect. When the officer found Michael hitchhiking, he mistakenly believed he was picking up the sexual assault suspect rather than a murder suspect. Michael vaguely resembled the description of the sexual assault suspect. He was picked up, handcuffed, put into the police car, and driven to the police station, where he was put into a police lineup with five other men. When the victim didn't choose him out of the lineup, Michael Bear was released without charge.

Two days later, police realized the arresting officer had made yet another important mistake: he had failed to properly search Michael before he put him in the squad car. Michael had hidden a handgun in between the seat cushions in the back of the car.

When police looked back at the record from the day of his arrest, they noticed that he claimed to have no driver's license and provided a name and address in Arizona. The name he provided was neither Michael Bear nor James Carson. Thinking he was being clever, Michael had given the name and address of Suzan's ex-husband in Scottsdale, Arizona.

When detectives contacted Suzan's ex-husband and showed him the arrest photo, he told them they were looking for a man named James Carson, who also went by the name Michael Bear. After a bit of research, detectives matched the arrest photo to the composite sketch from the Northern California killing of Clarke Stephens. It was then that they realized they had just released a murderer.

Several more months passed and Michael and Suzan were making their way to Santa Rosa, California, along Highway 101 when Charles Hillyar pulled his truck over to the side of the road and offered the couple a ride. With Suzan sitting in the middle and Michael on the passenger side, the problems started almost immediately.

Hillyar's leg brushed against Suzan's and she flew into a rage. She screamed that he had sexually abused her. Suzan then told Michael that the good Samaritan that had just given them a ride was a witch and had to die.

Hillyar pulled the truck to the side of the road and Michael attacked. Hillyar and Michael both got out of the truck and the fight continued on the side of the highway for almost ten minutes, with passing motorists slowing down to watch. The fight ended, however, when Suzan found a gun beneath the seat of the truck, handed it to Michael, and screamed, "Kill the witch!"

Michael shot and killed Hillyar, who fell to the ground in full view of several passing motorists. Michael and Suzan fled in the truck while witnesses called the police. Michael and Suzan Bear led police on a high-speed chase until they finally crashed into a ditch on a dead-end road in Napa County.

——

After their arrest, Michael and Suzan Bear told detectives that they would only speak to them under one condition: they wanted an audience. If police agreed to a televised press conference, they would tell them everything they wanted to know. Prosecutors agreed and a press conference was arranged for April 12, 1983.

Michael and Suzan kissed, hugged, smiled, and laughed when the television cameras hit their faces. They had nothing to hide and held nothing back. For more than five hours, the two of them rambled on with deranged conspiracy theories of witches and demons and explained their unhinged views of the world.

Suzan & Michael Bear at televised press conference

They detailed how they had killed Keryn Barnes because Suzan had received orders to kill her from God during a rainstorm.

"Each time Suzan said that Keryn should be killed, the thunder would clap," claimed Michael.

He went on to explain the sounds of the blood gurgling from her neck when he stabbed her and how he hit her head as hard as he could with the frying pan. They claimed Keryn was a "religious faker" and had "faked her conversion to Islam and was secretly draining Suzan of her mystical powers."

They laughed and smiled and told the cameras that they had been doing the world a favor by getting rid of witches. They said Ronald Wilson Reagan had to die because each of his names had six letters in it, meaning that he was a demon that bore the mark of the beast: six-six-six. Michael continued, "I had no choice but to commit the murders. It was part of the Koran."

Suzan spoke at length about her psychic abilities and how she and Michael had actually met several other times in their past lives, once in the Middle Ages and again in ancient Egypt. She had been searching in this life for her one true love and had found him once again in Michael Bear.

———

Michael and Suzan Bear believed that there was no such thing as coincidence and all objects in the universe were linked by a mystical principle. They believed they were Islamic warriors chosen by God. Michael spoke of his knowledge of karate and how he was preparing to use it to fight the Russians and the darkness that was sweeping across America.

Suzan believed that eyeglasses were evil because they interfered with the soul's third eye. Therefore, she refused to let Michael wear his glasses when driving despite his horrible vision.

Suzan also had strange views of Charles Manson. Manson never actually killed anyone and instead had his followers do his dirty work. Suzan believed that made him a "low-class criminal" that was unwilling to get his own hands dirty. She often encouraged Michael to be less like Manson and to do the killings himself.

———

Despite the public press conference, Michael and Suzan Bear entered pleas of not guilty just before their trial. In June 1984, they were convicted on all three counts of first-degree murder. They both received twenty-five years in prison for the murder of Keryn Barnes. They received an additional fifty years for the murder of Clarke Stephens and seventy-five years to life for the murder of Charles Hillyar.

Jennifer Carson, the daughter of Michael Bear / James Carson, finally visited her father in prison years later in 1997, where he rambled conspiracy nonsense for three hours. She told reporters afterward, "My daddy's not in there anymore."

In 2020, 1,400 elderly inmates received early parole hearings due to California's overcrowded prisons. Suzan Bear didn't appear for her hearing. Michael, too, denied his chance at parole, telling prison officials, "No one is going to parole me because I will not and have not renounced my beliefs."

The Bears remain suspects in nearly a dozen other murders throughout the United States and Europe.

CHAPTER 13
BONUS CHAPTER: THE FAMILY MURDERS

T his chapter is a **free bonus chapter** from True Crime
Case Histories: Volume 7

———

The River Torrens flows from the peaks of Mount Pleasant,
through the Adelaide Hills, to the Adelaide Plains and supplies
water to the city center of Adelaide, Australia, before it
continues into Gulf St. Vincent.

In the early 1970s, the area where the river flows through the
base of the foothills was a popular "beat" for gay men to meet.
Homosexuality was illegal at the time and South Australia's Vice
Squad regularly patrolled the area.

In May 1972, corrupt police officers confronted three gay men,
Roger James, Dr. George Duncan, and another man. Rather
than cite the men for their crimes, the officers threw them in
the rapid waters of River Torrens and left them to drown.
Throwing gay men into the river was a common occurrence
among the Vice Squad who considered it a "sport" and referred
to the act as "flinging a poof."

Dr. George Duncan, a law lecturer at Adelaide University, drowned in the incident and was found 500 meters downstream. His death made him a martyr for gay rights activists in the area and the event helped repeal South Australia's anti-homosexuality laws.

The other two men were rescued that night with the help of a young man that was driving by. The young man was Bevan Spencer von Einem. von Einem drove the two men to the hospital and became a hero in Southern Australia. Although von Einem's first media appearance made him a hero, years later, he would return to the spotlight for much more sinister reasons.

———

Seven years later, sixteen-year-old Alan Barnes had spent the night at a friend's house in Adelaide. The following morning, a Sunday in June 1979, the teenager walked to Grand Junction Road to see if he could hitch a ride home. Hitchhiking had been common in the area at the time and was generally a safe way to get around the city. Although Alan was due home that Sunday afternoon, his parents allowed the boy his independence and didn't think too much of it when he hadn't returned home that day. When he hadn't arrived by Monday morning, however, Alan's mother knew something was wrong and called police.

Alan had long, blonde hair that stood out in a crowd. When police questioned people in the area, several remembered seeing him hitchhiking, but only one could provide any useful information. A motorist that had been driving on Grand Junction Road that morning claimed to have seen Alan getting into a car with three or four people. Unfortunately, the person was unable to give a description of the car or its passengers.

The following Sunday, just one week after Alan went missing, a couple hiking in the Adelaide Foothills near the South Para Reservoir came across an object along a trail beneath a bridge. As they approached, they could tell it was the body of a young male. The body had been twisted and contorted.

When police arrived, they found the body of a boy they believed to be in his twenties. It appeared someone had thrown the body over the railing of the bridge above, hoping it would land in the water. Instead, the body hit the dirt.

The news reports that evening announced that the body of a young man in his twenties was found deceased. When Alan's mother heard the news, she knew it had to be her son. She called police and said, "He's not in his twenties. He's sixteen. And if you look at the back of his watch, you'll see an engraving. It was his Christmas present."

It was indeed Alan. A postmortem examination of his body showed that he had died on Friday night or Saturday morning, just hours before he was dumped. Since he had been gone a week, that left the last six days of his life unaccounted for. His body had been meticulously washed clean in an attempt to hide evidence and he had been dressed in clothes that were not his own.

A toxicology examination revealed a large dose of a potent sedative called Noctec in his system. The condition of his body led police to believe that he had been drugged, severely beaten, brutally tortured, and held captive in the days before his death. Alan had died from massive blood loss in and around his anus. He had been raped with a large object, believed to be a bottle, which perforated the inside of his rectum. Clearly, it was the work of a psychotic sexual sadist.

———

Two months later, in August 1979, a man fishing from a dock at Mutton Cove, just Northwest of Adelaide, noticed a pair of black trash bags floating in the water along the bank of the Port Adelaide River. Curious, he opened one of the bags and called police when he saw what looked like butchered human remains inside.

The bags had been placed in the water just a mile from where the river flowed into the ocean. The killer assumed the current would carry the bags into the open sea, but they had caught on a dock.

When detectives opened the bag, it was enough to bring seasoned officers to tears. The first bag contained a male torso with the chest cavity cut open. The organs had been removed from the torso and placed into smaller plastic bags. The severed legs and arms had been stripped of skin and muscle tissue and placed into the chest cavity. The head had been severed from the body and strangely wired to the chest.

A medical examination determined the victim died in a similar manner to Alan Barnes. He had been tortured and bled to death from anal injuries. He had been brutally raped with a bottle-shaped object which had perforated his rectum and anus. There was evidence of blunt force trauma to his head, but not enough to have caused death.

Alan Barnes / Neil Muir

The body was identified as Neil Muir, a twenty-five-year-old gay heroin user that was well known to police. Neil lived alone and had only been reported missing two days before the body was found. Detectives weren't quite sure how long he had been missing. Like Alan Barnes, Neil had been last seen on a Sunday. Both bodies had been discarded in or near water and both had died of blood loss from anal injuries. Though the similarities seem glaringly obvious in hindsight, the two murders weren't initially linked together.

———

Shortly after the body of Neil Muir was discovered, police received an anonymous phone call from someone that referred to himself as "Mr. B." The caller told detectives he believed that Bevan Spencer von Einem was responsible for the murders. von Einem's name was added to a list of leads, along with hundreds of others.

When detectives interviewed von Einem, he freely admitted
that he knew Neil Muir. The two of them had been lovers four
years earlier. von Einem claimed to have met with Neil a few
days before he went missing, but hadn't seen him since.
Although it was a significant finding, the information was lost
in the hundreds of other leads detectives needed to follow
up on.

———

Two years had gone by with very little development in either
murder. On February 27, 1982, nineteen-year-old Mark
Langley attended a friend's birthday party. After the party, he
and two friends went for a drive through the city. As they drove
near the River Torrens, Mark had an argument with his friends,
got out of the car, and told them he would walk home. Mark's
friends drove off, but it had been a petty argument and, just
minutes later, his friends had a change of heart. They turned
around to pick him up, but Mark was nowhere to be found.
Assuming he had found a ride home, they went home without
him.

The following morning, Mark's father called the police to
report him missing. Mark's friends and family searched the area
where he was last seen, but he had simply vanished. Divers
were sent to search the River Torrens but found nothing. Nine
days after Mark went missing, his body was found in an area
called Summertown at the base of Mount Lofty, just east of
Adelaide.

Unlike the other victims, Mark's body had no visible external
injuries. His clothes were clean, but his blue undershirt was
missing, as was his silver necklace with a zodiac pendant. He
died, however, just like the others—from massive blood loss due
to injuries to his anus and rectum caused by the insertion of a

bottle-shaped object. Also, similar to Alan Barnes, Mark's body had been washed clean before it was dumped.

Strangely, Mark's body had a small, recent, vertical surgical scar. Someone had performed surgery on him just below his navel, even taking the time to shave him before surgery. The wound was stitched closed with surgical thread and Johnson & Johnson surgical tape afterwards. Medical examiners and investigators believed the surgery was performed in order to retrieve an object that may have been caught in his intestines - possibly an object that the killer believed could have contained a fingerprint.

Like the victims before, Mark had been given alcohol and a massive amount of a sedative called Mandrax, more widely known as methaqualone or quaalude.

Detectives finally began to consider the possibility that the three murders were linked. As a result, they began looking into other missing person cases that may also have been related. That's when they noticed the case file of Peter Stogneff.

———

On August 27, 1981, exactly six months before Mark Langley's disappearance, fourteen-year-old Peter Stogneff made plans with a friend to skip school. Before he left home that morning, he dropped his school backpack in his garage and took the bus into the city to meet his friend. Peter's friend waited patiently at the local shopping mall, but Peter never showed. Later that evening, when Peter didn't return home, his parents called the police to report him missing. An extensive search ensued, but Peter had vanished without a trace. The only clue was a witness at Tea Tree Plaza that claimed they saw the boy with an adult male.

Almost a year later in a small town just north of Adelaide, a farmer conducting a burn-off (a fire-management process used to encourage plant growth and reduce wildfires) discovered a human skeleton in the ashes. Unfortunately, any evidence that may have been at the scene was now charred. Using dental records, investigators determined it was the remains of Peter Stogneff. Although they were unable to determine an official cause of death, medical examiners could tell that the spine had been severed with a saw and his legs had been sawed just above the knees.

———

For the next fifteen months, the cases went nowhere. Police briefly thought they had found the killer: Dr. Peter Millhouse, a doctor who had known Neil Muir. Prosecutors brought a case against the man based on weak circumstantial evidence, but at trial he was easily acquitted. They were back to square one.

———

On a Sunday afternoon in July 1983, fifteen-year-old Richard Kelvin and his friend Boris were at a local park kicking around a soccer ball. Richard was a handsome, athletic boy with a steady girlfriend and got good grades in school. That afternoon, as a joke, he wore the family dog's collar around his neck as he played with Boris in the park.

Peter Stogneff / Richard Kelvin

When it was time to go home, the two boys walked to the bus stop and Richard waited as Boris caught his bus home. Richard began his walk home, less than a quarter of a mile from the bus stop, but he never made it. He had simply disappeared.

The case of Richard Kelvin's disappearance drew more attention in the media than the other cases. Richard was the son of a well-known local newscaster that worked for Channel 9. Richard had been wearing a Channel 9 t-shirt when he disappeared.

Initially, local police assumed Richard had simply run away from home. His frustrated parents protested and explained that Richard was a good kid; he would never run away from home. Police had wasted two days and Richard still hadn't returned home. That Tuesday, police finally began a door-to-door search of the area and came up with a clue.

A man living nearby that worked as a security guard told police that on the Sunday evening when Richard went missing, he heard shouting on the street near his home. He said he could hear arguing, cries for help, and car doors slamming on the street nearby. One voice sounded young, several others were adults, and one voice appeared to be that of a woman. Immediately after the argument, he heard the loud exhaust of a car speeding away. By the time he looked outside, the car was gone. Other neighbors in the area corroborated the same story. It appeared as though a group of people had abducted Richard.

The location from which Richard was abducted was just a few blocks from where Mark Langley was last seen. Police and media immediately suspected that Richard may have been abducted by the same killer or killers as the other four victims. Theories arose that he possibly was abducted by sexual deviants because of the dog collar he wore around his neck.

Because of Richard's high-profile father, the story became front-page news. Everyone in the area seemed to have theories about what had happened and the police were inundated with calls. Anonymous callers told police he was being held in a camper near the mountains while others claimed to have seen his death in a snuff film.

Finally, seven weeks after Richard vanished, a family walking through the forest near Mount Crawford, northeast of Adelaide, came across what they thought was someone lying in the bushes in a fetal position. The father assumed it may be a man that was injured, but it soon became obvious that it was a dead body. As soon as the man noticed his Channel 9 shirt and the dog collar, he knew it was the body of Richard Kelvin.

An autopsy revealed exactly the same cause of death as the others: massive blood loss from anal injuries. His body had been washed clean and redressed in his own clothes. Richard, however, had been missing for much longer than the others. The state of decomposition revealed that he had been dead for only a week in the scrub brush. That meant that Richard had endured five to six weeks of excruciating torture and sexual abuse before his death.

Like the others, Richard's body contained a massive cocktail of powerful sedatives including Noctec (Chloral Hydrate), Mandrax (Quaalude), Valium (Diazepam), Rohypnol (roofies), and Amobarbital. It was clear to detectives that all five deaths were linked.

———

Six months prior to Richard Kelvin's murder, a young man named George informed police he had been kidnapped, drugged, and raped by several people. He told detectives that while hitchhiking, he was picked up by an older man who offered him alcohol in the backseat of his car and enticed him to come to a nearby house to drink with some older women. At the house, the women flirted with him and gave him more alcohol. After some time, he began feeling drowsy and the last thing he remembered was being taken into a bedroom to have sex with one of the women. Just before he blacked out, he realized that the woman was not female, but a transvestite.

George woke up the next day in his own home, but crippled with pain and no recollection of the rest of the night or how he got home. He went to the police to report the incident and agreed to a medical and toxicological test. He had severe lacerations in his anus and his blood contained a significant quantity of Mandrax. It was the same drug that was found in the systems of Richard Kelvin and Mark Langley.

Detectives searched through prior police reports and found many similar stories. There were several other young men that had also been abducted, drugged, and raped.

Mandrax had become a popular recreational drug in the late 1970s, known on the street as "Randy Mandys." It was a date-rape drug. This led the South Australia government to regulate it and several other drugs. After its regulation, every prescription of the drug had a paper trail and police believed their best option was to search for who had access to these drugs.

Detectives took the time to sift through thousands of records of individuals in South Australia that had been prescribed Mandrax. After extensive searches, the name Bevan Spencer von Einem came up.

———

Bevan Spencer von Einem

At first appearance, von Einem seemed normal enough. He was in his late thirties, prematurely gray, worked as an accountant, and still lived with his mother. Detectives questioned von Einem at his workplace and at home without prior notice. They wanted to surprise him and not give him the opportunity to prepare his answers. When asked about his prescriptions, von Einem explained he was an insomniac and had trouble sleeping his entire life. He claimed the prescriptions for Mandrax and Rohypnol were to help him sleep. He flatly denied knowing any of the victims other than Neil Muir.

When asked about his whereabouts on the night Richard Kelvin was kidnapped, he had an answer prepared. He claimed he was home sick with the flu the entire week and his mother could back up his story.

von Einem seemed to have prepared answers for every question, often giving racist comments baselessly suggesting that people like Lebanese, Greek, or Italian immigrants must have committed the murders. When asked point-blank if he had committed the murders, he gave a strange response, telling the detectives,

"No, of course not. That would be unethical."

———

Detectives tracked down the anonymous caller, "Mr. B," who had mentioned von Einem years earlier. He agreed to speak to detectives again on the condition that he could remain anonymous. Mr. B was in his early twenties, which meant he would have been a teenager when he associated with von Einem. He claimed he would ride with von Einem while he drove around Adelaide, picking up young boys on the streets. The men would offer boys a ride and give them alcohol from a cooler that von Einem always kept in the back seat of his car. After a few drinks, the boys were invited to a party with more alcohol and women. von Einem would then offer the boys what he told them was "NoDoz", a popular caffeine pill at the time. But rather than caffeine, the pills were actually one of his powerful sedatives.

After the boys had passed out from the sedatives, Mr. B claimed von Einem would take the boys to a house owned by two transgender women, where they would be raped by multiple men, often with a bottle. Afterwards, most of them would be released with only a vague recollection of what had happened to them.

Mr. B's explanation was virtually the same as what the young man, George, had told them. Although police were glad to have the information about von Einem, they believed that Mr. B had more involvement than he was admitting. The young man had been careful not to implicate himself, however, and claimed to have witnessed the events, but never participated.

————

In the Fall of 1983, investigators searched von Einem's home he shared with his mother. Although there was no evidence of a murder having happened at the residence, they did find his prescription for Mandrax in his bathroom. He claimed that was the only drug he had, but when police continued their search, several more drugs were found in a duffel bag. Even more were hidden on a secret ledge hidden behind his closet. The drugs were the same that had been found in the bodies of the victims: Noctec, Valium, and Rohypnol. Samples were also taken of von Einem's hair and blood.

On the evening after the search of von Einem's home, detectives parked nearby and watched as a man who would later become known as "Mr. R" visited von Einem. Mr. R was a businessman in Adelaide and a close friend of von Einem. The man remained at the house for several hours.

————

Bevan Spencer von Einem was arrested and charged with the murder of Richard Kelvin on November 3, 1983. Prosecutors believed the link between the drugs found in Richard Kelvin's body and the drugs found in von Einem's home was enough to convict him for that murder. The other four murders would have to wait.

Over the next several months, detectives gathered evidence. Of the 925 fibers found on Richard Kelvin's clothing, 250 of them came from von Einem's bedroom carpet, bedspread, and cardigan sweater. von Einem's hairs were found inside Richard's jeans.

Between December 1978 and August 1983, von Einem had been prescribed 5,873 tablets and capsules of the six different types of sedatives, often filling the prescriptions from three different pharmacists on the same day.

———

Police believed that von Einem murdered all five boys, but he wasn't alone. He had to have had help. Neil Muir had been butchered in such a way that they believed someone with surgery experience was involved. The same experience would have been needed for the surgery that was done to Mark Langley. There were accounts of several people in a car abducting Richard Kelvin, while additional accounts pointed toward several other men involved in the rapes, as well as transgender women.

Investigators searched a building owned by von Einem's associate, Mr. R, in central Adelaide. The entire second floor of the building was vacant, with only a mattress lying on the floor. Police believed this could have been a location they used to rape the young boys.

Mr. R was a gay man that was known to spend his lunch breaks cruising gay areas of Adelaide looking for young men. His roommate was a doctor named Stephen George Woodwards. Woodwards had been accused multiple times of sexual assault, eventually facing charges. Police believed Woodwards could have performed the surgery that was done to Mark Langley.

Although detectives were able to show that von Einem ran in the same circles as these men, they had trouble directly linking them to any of the crimes.

———

With the discovery of the fibers and hairs on Richard Kelvin's clothes, von Einem changed his story. Initially, he had claimed he was sick with the flu for a full week during Richard's disappearance. He even had a prescription filled. Now he claimed he had been driving in the area to get some fish and chips when he encountered Richard Kelvin. He told detectives he struck up a conversation with Richard and the fifteen-year-old boy came with him willingly. He claimed they drove around the city and talked. Richard spoke to him at length about school problems and girlfriend problems. von Einem claimed he then brought Richard back to his home, where they talked some more. He said that at one point he put his arm around Richard, which he explained as the reason that fibers from his cardigan were found on Richard's clothes. He claimed that the carpet fibers on Richard's body were from when he sat on the floor while von Einem played the harp for him. von Einem then explained that he gave Richard $20 for a taxi ride back home and that was the last he had seen of him.

Detectives didn't buy his story for a minute. The fibers from von Einem's carpet and his own hairs were found on the inside of Richard's clothing, not the outside. Also, Richard had died five weeks after he went missing. Any such fibers from the day he went missing would have been gone by that amount of time.

More importantly, von Einem had just admitted that he was the last person to see Richard alive. Despite the evidence against him, von Einem pleaded not-guilty.

Bevan Spencer von Einem's trial started on October 15, 1984. His defense tried to imply that Richard Kelvin was secretly bisexual, which wasn't true, and ultimately didn't make a difference to their case. von Einem was found guilty on November 5 after less than eight hours of deliberation. The conviction came with an automatic life sentence with parole eligibility in twenty-four years. Eight of those years could be taken off for good behavior.

von Einem could conceivably have been released in as little as sixteen years. The Attorney General, however, filed an immediate appeal to lengthen the parole period. As a result, his parole eligibility was extended to thirty-six years.

The first guest to visit von Einem in jail was Mr. R

———

In the years after von Einem's conviction, detectives searched for evidence to convict von Einem or any accomplices for the additional four murders. A $250,000 reward was offered for information leading to an arrest and over time the reward was gradually increased to $1,000,000, but with no results.

Mr. B continued to provide the prosecution with information claiming that von Einem and Mr. R had made a snuff film of the killing of Alan Barnes. He also told police that von Einem had been involved in the Beaumont Children's disappearance in 1966, as well as the disappearance of two girls from an Australian rules football match in 1973. Of course, the accusations were just Mr. B's word without actual evidence.

Mr. B's sister contacted police and claimed that her brother once told her he had participated in the abduction and murder of a young man in Adelaide. She claimed they threw the body off a bridge. Again, without actual evidence.

By 1990, armed only with circumstantial evidence, prosecutors brought von Einem back to trial for the murders of Alan Barnes and Mark Langley. In a massive blow to the prosecution, much of the evidence presented, however, was deemed inadmissible by the court. In order to avoid a possible acquittal, the charges were eventually dropped.

———

One of the detectives working the case appeared on the television news show "60 Minutes." During the show, he spoke of his desire to break up "the happy family," referring to his belief that there were many more people helping von Einem commit the crimes. He believed there was evidence linking wealthy Adelaide businessmen, politicians, judges, and doctors, all child sex abusers.

Over the next few decades, the case remained the subject of conspiracy theories throughout South Australia. Many people believed to have been involved remain with their identity hidden, while others have been revealed.

———

Mr. R - Known to be a longtime friend of von Einem and visited him in prison multiple times. Police have long suspected him as an accomplice to the murders but were unable to produce evidence.

Dr. Stephen Woodwards - Woodwards refused to answer questions to police. Investigators believed he supplied von Einem with drugs and may have helped butcher the victims, as well as sexually assaulting them.

Denis St Denis - Another of von Einem's longtime friends as well as his hairdresser. Police believe Richard Kelvin was held at St Denis' home while he was tortured and killed.

Mr. B - Although he was careful not to implicate himself when questioned by police, detectives believe he was involved in many of the abductions.

Prudence Firman - A transgender woman who had a sex change in 1982 is believed to have allowed use of her home for abductions in exchange for drugs.

Noel Terrance Brooks - Was believed to have been seen with Peter Stogneff on the day he disappeared.

Derrance Stevenson - A high profile lawyer that was an associate of Alan Barnes. Stevenson dealt heroin from his home and was known for his predilection for young boys. He was murdered by his nineteen-year-old lover, David Szach, just weeks after Alan's murder.

Gino Gambardella - Fled Australia to Italy after several accusations of sexual assault. He's a close friend of both von Einem and Stevenson.

The list of suspected involved parties goes on and on.

Another gay man with an association to von Einem was Trevor Peters. After his death in 2014, his family found a diary as they sifted through his belongings.

Entries in the diary discussed his relationship with von Einem in detail and several others listed above. The diary alleged that von Einem had discussed the abduction of Alan Barnes with his hairdresser, Denis St Denis, and laughed about taking photos of Barnes as he was being held captive.

Another person implicated in the diary was Lewis Turtur. Turtur was well-known as a flamboyant drag queen whose brother was a famous Olympic athlete. When news crews confronted Turtur about his association with von Einem, Turtur admitted his involvement and admitted to abducting boys, but insisted he had nothing to do with the murders.

> "All I know is they came in… he dropped them off at our place, he went home, we let them sleep it off, they left in the morning. I was a stupid fool, wasn't I? Half the time I was drugged out anyway, so I don't really care. I was in my own little world."

Investigators believe there may have been as many as 150 abductions and many more murders throughout the years that have been unreported or unlinked. Although many associates of von Einem, all with a passion for young boys, were believed to have been involved, none have ever been charged.

———

This chapter is a free bonus chapter from True Crime Case Histories: Volume 7

Online Appendix

Visit my website for additional photos and videos pertaining to the cases in this book:

http://TrueCrimeCaseHistories.com/vol9/

More books by Jason Neal

Looking for more?? I am constantly adding new volumes of True Crime Case Histories. The series **can be read in any order,** and all books are also available in paperback, hardcover, and audiobook.

Check out the complete series on Amazon

https://amazon.com/author/jason-neal

or

JasonNealBooks.com

**FREE Bonus Book
For My Readers**

**Click to get
your free copy!**

As my way of saying "Thank you" for downloading, I'm giving away a FREE true crime book I think you'll enjoy.

https://TrueCrimeCaseHistories.com

Just click the link above to let me know where to send your free book!

Choose Your Free True Crime Audiobook

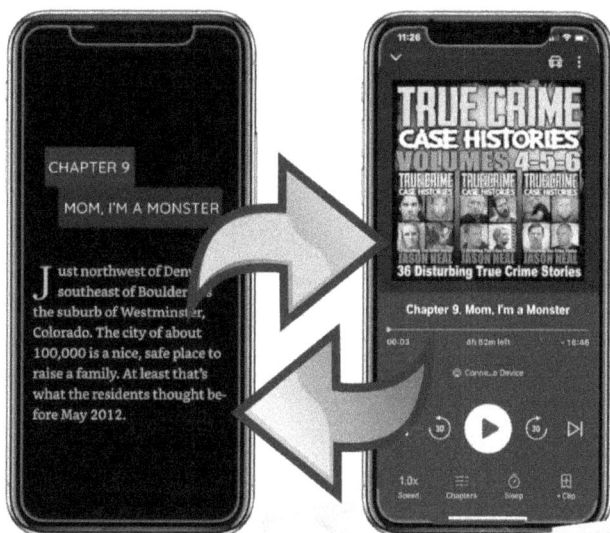

Add Audible Narration and Keep the Story Going!
Plus Get a FREE True Crime Audiobook!

Switch between listening to an audiobook and reading on your Kindle.
Plus choose your first audiobook for FREE!

https://geni.us/AudibleTrueCrime

THANK YOU!

Thank you for reading this Volume of True Crime Case Histories. I truly hope you enjoyed it. If you did, I would be sincerely grateful if you would take a few minutes to write a review for me on Amazon using the link below.

https://geni.us/TrueCrime9

I'd also like to encourage you to sign-up for my email list for updates, discounts and freebies on future books! I promise I'll make it worth your while with future freebies.

http://truecrimecasehistories.com

And please take a moment and follow me on Amazon.

One last thing. As I mentioned previously, many of the stories in this series were suggested to me by readers like you. I like to feature stories that many true crime fans haven't heard of, so if there's a story that you remember from the past that you haven't seen covered by other true crime sources, please send me any details you can remember and I will do my best to research it. Or if you'd like to contact me for any other reason free to email me at:

jasonnealbooks@gmail.com

https://linktr.ee/JasonNeal

Thanks so much,

Jason Neal

ABOUT THE AUTHOR

Jason Neal is a Best-Selling American True Crime Author living in Hawaii with his Turkish-British wife. Jason started his writing career in the late eighties as a music industry publisher and wrote his first true crime collection in 2019.

As a boy growing up in the eighties just south of Seattle, Jason became interested in true crime stories after hearing the news of the Green River Killer so close to his home. Over the subsequent years he would read everything he could get his hands on about true crime and serial killers.

As he approached 50, Jason began to assemble stories of the crimes that have fascinated him most throughout his life. He's especially obsessed by cases solved by sheer luck, amazing police work, and groundbreaking technology like early DNA cases and more recently reverse genealogy.